Every ble

CH00642724

R. B. JONES

R. B. Jones

Gospel ministry
in turbulent times

Noel Gibbard

BRYNTIRION PRESS

© Noel Gibbard
First published 2009

ISBN: 978 1 85049 231 3

Cover design: Creative Media Ltd.

Published by Bryntirion Press
Bryntirion, Bridgend CF31 4DX, Wales, UK

Printed by Gomer Press, Llandysul, Ceredigion SA44 4JL

To
Hebron Evangelical Church, Dowlais,
where R. B. Jones was brought up,
and to
Ainon Welsh Baptist Church, Ynys-hir, and
Tabernacle Baptist Church, Porth,
where he ministered for twenty-nine years
(Ainon, 1904–1919; Tabernacle, 1919–1933)

Contents

Preface

RHYS BEVAN JONES was an influential and a controversial character. He was both widely respected and bitterly criticised. It is surprising that no place was found for him in the *Dictionary of Welsh Biography*, and that T. M. Bassett in his work *The Welsh Baptists* devoted to him just one, misleading, sentence. There is clear need to trace the story of his life and assess his contribution to the religious life of Wales.

I am indebted to the published work of the late Rev. Brynmor Pierce Jones of Newport. He also collected a great deal of material relating to the Revival of 1904–5, and deposited it at the National Library of Wales, Aberystwyth. I have made much use of this collection and, during my visits to the Library, found members of staff very helpful.

Mr Eben Phillips of Ynys-hir, Rhondda, kindly sent me a copy of *Llyfryn Coffa Ainon, Ynyshir, 1880–1914*. Three churches gave financial help: the Welsh Evangelical Church, Cardiff; Hebron Evangelical Church, Dowlais, and Tabernacle Baptist Church, Porth. Their contribution is much appreciated. Mr David Jones, Secretary of Tabernacle, was personally supportive, and helped me in matters relating to the Church. In the light of the link between Porth, Barry and Bryntirion, it is significant that the present pastor of Tabernacle was trained at the Evangelical Theological College of Wales, Bryntirion, as it was known in his student days. (It is now called Wales Evangelical School of Theology.)

My thanks are due to both Dr Eifion Evans and Dr Huw Walters for their willingness to write a commendation of the work. I am grateful to Dr John Aaron and Miss Brenda Lewis for preparing the work for the press, and to Mr Edmund Owen who compiled the Index.

NOEL GIBBARD
Cardiff

May 2009

1
Early days and early ministries

In 1841, Caersalem Welsh Baptist Church in Dowlais, Merthyr Tydfil, obtained land from the Dowlais Iron Works, owned by Sir Josiah John Guest, to build a new chapel.[1] It was named Hebron and was opened in 1843, becoming independent of Caersalem in 1846. Its 106 members were constituted as an independent church on 23-24 May 1846. Four services were held during the inaugural meetings, with two preachers in each service.[2] The mention of both iron works and chapel is a reminder that in Dowlais at that time, as in Merthyr Tydfil, two things were inescapable—'smoke and chapels, industry and prayer, labour and religion'.[3]

Caeharris

Hebron was located at the centre of Caeharris, a small close-knit community of about a thousand inhabitants.[4] It was surrounded by signs of development, both social and industrial. Sir John owned not only the Iron Works but also the Ivor Works nearby, to the west of Caeharris, and named after his son. Sir John and his wife, Lady Charlotte Guest (famous for translating the oldest Welsh legends, the *Mabinogion*, into English), contributed in other ways to the welfare of Dowlais. 'Dowlais Parish Church, the Old Central Schools and the Guest Memorial Library became public testimonies to the couple's generosity.'[5] All these buildings were within a few hundred yards of Hebron.

Just below Hebron was the entrance to Caeharris Railway Station, where colliers and ironworkers would arrive from the Bargoed area and proceed by various lines to the collieries and iron works.[6] Transport to Merthyr was by means of freight train, or by a horse-drawn carriage costing sixpence (6d) per journey. For most of the people of Dowlais that price was too high, and it was a great boon, therefore, when a passenger train started to run between the two places.[7] To the north of Hebron chapel, the Abergavenny–Merthyr line passed through Dowlais Top. A bridge carried this railway over the Dowlais–Abergavenny road, and it was in the shadow of this bridge that Rhys Bevan Jones was born in 1869. His parents, also born in Dowlais, were John Jones, an engine fitter, and Mary (neé Bevan).[8] Rhys was born at home—64 Caeharris. His first impressions would have been of rumbling trains, the security of home, and the fellowship at Hebron Church, less than two hundreds yards down the road.

John and Mary Jones eventually had seven children, two of whom died in infancy, but Rhys was their first-born. He was still the only child in 1871, by which time there were six people living in the house. With so many men migrating into the area for work, many families took in lodgers. The Jones family received a stonemason from Leominster, together with his wife from Hanley and their seven-month-old son.[9] Another aspect of community life in Dowlais was the presence of the extended family. A few doors away from the Jones family, for example, lived the Rossers: husband, wife, three daughters, and the husbands of two of the daughters.[10]

In the streets around Caeharris Station lived many Irishmen, a number of whom were lodgers. They were regular visitors to The Red Bull, a public house immediately across the road from Hebron. The chapel and the public house challenged each other for supremacy in Caeharris, doing so with increasing intensity as the Temperance Movement flourished. The Red Bull received support even from some of the chapel members. There is a story of one member emerging from the Red Bull just as the minister was coming out of Hebron. The latter rebuked his wandering sheep. 'Drunk again, Davy', he said, and received the reply, 'And me too. Lovely, isn't it?'[11] But with respect to temperance there was no uncertainty in the Jones household; John Jones was a teetotaller.

Rhys's father was of small stature physically, but he possessed an independent mind. His only reading was of the Bible and a few religious books. He had been converted in 1859 and appointed a deacon of Hebron in 1877. Later, in 1884, he became secretary of the church.[12] A skilled engine fitter, he eventually became the overman (supervisor) of the fitting shop in the Iron Works. His wages were twenty-five shillings (£1.25p) a week. Though not a fluent speaker, he was respected for his knowledge and was sometimes asked to deliver lectures at the local Institute.[13]

John Jones's heart was in Hebron. Had he been a railwayman, the request and promise of the Taff Vale Railway Company would have held no attraction for him. The Company had declared: 'It is urgently requested every person . . . on Sunday and Holy Days, when he is not required on duty, that he will attend a place of worship; as it will be the means of promotion when vacancies occur.'[14] John Jones was strong-willed. For him, worship came before work, and principle before promotion. His wife Mary, a daughter of the well-known Bevan family of Dowlais, was known for her kindness and graciousness.

John Jones, Berry Square, the grandfather on the paternal side, had a marked influence on R. B. Jones. He was a devout person who had a calming influence on his neigh-bours. For instance, during storms of thunder and light-ning they would check to see if John Jones were at home. If so, they would be happy; conversely, his absence would make them nervous. He was regarded as eccentric in some things: he would not allow anyone to take his photograph, for example, and was reluctant to have his hair trimmed.[15]

Education

As regards education, R. B. Jones was very fortunate to be born in Dowlais. Sir John Guest was concerned for the education of his workers and their families, and his first school was opened in 1814.[16] That building became the stables for the works, but other schools were built during the period 1814–55. Further developments took place in 1855, when Lady Charlotte Guest opened new schools for infants, juniors and seniors. There was provision also for other age groups in evening classes. Two further signifi-cant changes affected these schools. First of all, they began to receive government grants, which were then supple-mented by the Guest Works; and secondly, they were taken over as British and Foreign Schools, a move which reflected the strength of Nonconformity in Dowlais. Previously they had been National Schools, where the Anglican Catechism was read and the Rector of Dowlais made supervisory visits.[17]

The headmaster of the Boys School from 1844 to 1892 was Matthew Hirst, a Yorkshireman. Education was paid for in two ways: by school pence and by poundage. The child of a workman would pay 2d a week, and the work-men would contribute ½d in the pound from their wages.[18] There were a few places for the children of tradesmen, and these paid 4d a week.

Classes were graded. The first class provided for those anxious to obtain a good position in the Iron Works, and the syllabus included arithmetic, algebra, mechanics, reading, writing and Scripture. The second class omitted such subjects as algebra and mechanics, and the third class was confined to elementary education.[19] Rhys most probably attended the first class.

According to his nephew, when Rhys Jones left school he began surface work at a colliery where his grandfather worked. This involved getting up very early for breakfast at 5.30 a.m. During the meal his grandfather would read from the Scriptures and pray. Rhys cherished those prayers throughout his life. Then, after a brief period in the colliery he found work in the fitting shop in the Iron Works. Brynmor Pierce Jones, however, relates a different sequence of events. According to him, Rhys went from the Boys' School, Dowlais, to another school at Penydarren, and from there to the fitting shop. This is confirmed by Geraint, one of R. B. Jones's sons, and by William Joseph Rhys.[20] It is difficult therefore to be sure when it was that R. B. Jones worked in a colliery, as his nephew suggests.[21]

It was at this period, when he was about twelve years of age, that Rhys Jones committed himself to God and experienced forgiveness. His minister at this time was the Rev. O. W. James, who was very ready to help and advise him.[22] At the Merthyr Proprietary School, Penydarren, his teacher was T. C. Fawcett, MA, who was responsible for both boarders and day scholars.[23] It was fortunate that Rhys could be a day student, for the boarders had to pay from six to twelve guineas a year. His continuing studies in Mathematics confirmed the early steps taken at the Dowlais school and he won prizes for his work in this subject. These studies bore fruit later, as evidenced by his clear thinking and his organising ability.[24]

When he was eighteen years of age Rhys Jones went to Aberafan to receive further education from the Rev. T. Richards. One of his fellow students there was David Lloyd.[25] The two of them were to work together later during the 1904–5 Revival. Rhys was eventually accepted as a candidate for the ministry, and his choice of college was the Baptist College at Pontypool, under the presidency of the Rev. William Edwards.[26] During his first year in college, the Rev. Ceinfryn Thomas became minister at Hebron. This meant that the young student was now under the influence of two strong characters. Ceinfryn Thomas impressed him by his personal example and also by his insistence that preaching was the central work of the Christian ministry. The minister of Hebron was an influence not only upon his own church but upon the whole district. One historian has referred to him as 'the squarson' (squire-cum-parson).[27] William Edwards, like Ceinfryn Thomas, was well-known for his evangelicalism, and also for requiring high academic standards at Pontypool College.

There is little information on R. B. Jones's stay at the college. Some of his fellow students have suggested that he was 'arrogant and proud'.[28] He states himself that he was determined to do good to others and that he believed that his parents' advice, 'Watch and pray', would help him in this respect. Brynmor Pierce Jones refers to the significance of a photograph taken during this period:

> The deeper cause of being called seems to be more clearly expressed in a family album snapshot where a lean hawk-faced youth, in a smart box hat and well-tailored suit, carrying a preaching-bag, then of a new fashion, is bidding farewell to fellow students. He stands confidently at the gateway of the college, and of his new career.[29]

Berth-lwyd, Treharris

R. B. Jones had preached in Berth-lwyd Baptist Chapel, Treharris, during 1892, when that church was seeking a successor to Edward Jones (*Ieuan Ddu*). Before the end of that year he received a unanimous call from the church. He commenced his ministry on 1 January 1893, on a salary of £6 a month with four free Sundays in the year.[30] Like Dowlais, Treharris was an industrial area, but with a much smaller population.

From his first Sunday at the church, 'RB' (as he was familiarly known from very early on in his ministry) made clear his aim of preaching the gospel, and of preaching it with authority, whatever the response might be. His was to be the message of the mystery made known in Christ. This would require preaching of man's sin—that sin which had made necessary the coming of Christ into our world. God had revealed this mystery, for man's mind could never have discovered the truth for himself. And the gospel had been revealed in order for it to be proclaimed. There was a responsibility laid upon Berth-lwyd Church to be a praying church. This was essential for the ongoing work because of the nature of the gospel, because of the preacher's need, and because of the varying situations the church faced.[31] Prayer, preaching, and the unity of the church were the three essentials for the success of the gospel.

Together with this seriousness and direct presentation was a tendency at times to discuss matters that were not so helpful for the congregation. Thus, in one of his early sermons on Isaiah 55:10-11, his opening remark was, 'The text is an analogy.' He then referred to Butler's *Analogy of Religion*, commented on this book and spent some time explaining the word 'analogy'.[32]

RB's ministry at Berth-lwyd lasted only two years, but they were happy years. He gained experience, and he also married Lizzie Morgan, the niece of Alderman Llewelyn Griffiths of Cwmafan. She proved an immense help to him, both at home and in public.[33] In 1895, he received a call to the pastorate of Caersalem Baptist Chapel, Llanelli.

Caersalem, Llanelli

Caersalem had invited T. J. Evans, Rhydwilym, Pembroke-shire, to be their first minister. They had had to wait a long time before receiving a negative reply. In a subsequent meeting of the deacons on 18 January 1895, it was agreed to present the name of R. B. Jones, Berth-lwyd, to the church. The members already knew him as he had visited on several occasions. The church extended a unanimous call on 21 January 1895, and RB responded positively.[34] He was informed that the church would not be able to specify a salary but could assure him that it would not be less than £8 a month. Caersalem would also assume responsibility for moving the new pastor, and two deacons were appointed to travel to Berth-lwyd to supervise the arrangements.[35]

R. B. Jones arrived in Llanelli during April 1895. He attended a meeting of the Llanelli and District Baptist Union before commencing his ministry on the third Sunday of that month.[36] The induction service took place a few weeks later, presided over by Dr John Rhys Morgan (*Lleurwg*), Seion. A letter was read from the Rev. Ceinfryn Thomas, Dowlais, who was unable to attend, recommending the pastor as 'an able and godly young man'. A letter was also received from the Baptist Fellowship of Pontypridd and District.[37]

At this time, Llanelli was renowned for its large chapels, its busy tinplate works, and for Stradey Park, the popular Mecca of the rugby enthusiasts. A high percentage of the population attended public worship on Sunday and the public houses were closed on that day. There was a commitment to promoting Welsh culture, and the town was glad to welcome the National Eisteddfod in 1895. This event was held in the recently built Market Pavilion.

Many of Llanelli's ministers had a tremendous influence upon the town. Dr Morgan (*Lleurwg*), a preacher, lecturer and poet, had ministered in Llanelli for forty years.[38] The Rev. Trevor Jones had spent most of his ministerial life in Bethania Baptist Chapel and was later to work closely with RB in revival work, while Dr John Rowlands, Moriah, was renowned as a preacher and leader amongst the Baptists.[39] The Rev. Thomas Johns had already been ministering at Capel Als amongst the Congregationalists for twenty-six years. Like *Lleurwg*, he was a staunch Liberal and a member of the County Council. The Rev. D. Wynne Evans, Tabernacle (Congregationalist),[40] was much interested in the Holiness Movement and had attended the Keswick Conference in 1894. Later, in 1903, he was to be present with RB at the Keswick-in-Wales Conference, Llandrindod. One other minister must be mentioned. The Rev. W. S. Jones, Penuel (Baptist), Carmarthen, was to play an important part in RB's later life, but it was during this earlier period at Llanelli that their friendship was established.[41]

Caersalem Baptist Church was the daughter church of Bethel and Moriah. It was Bethel Church that had obtained the land on which to build the chapel, and a total of one hundred members from Bethel and Moriah, together with a few others from other churches, joined together to form a new cause. The total cost of the chapel, schoolroom and three houses on the site was £4,000. One of the houses became the manse for the minister. The Bethel church contributed £200 and the Moriah congregation £100.[42] These were worthy contributions, but it still took the church some years to clear their debt.

Although a young church, Caersalem was well organised. A diaconate and a secretary had been appointed, and these supervised closely the activities of overseers set over different areas. These overseers reported to the deacons and minister upon the needs of particular members, and they also reported the names of those who were neglecting the means of grace and those guilty of immorality. When RB arrived, the overseers presented him with a list of members who required a visit.[43]

R. B. Jones was happy with these arrangements. This is evident from the entries in the church registers. Soon after his arrival it was decided that a representative of the church should visit a particular member and ask him to be present at a Friday night church meeting. At that meeting he was to approach the big seat so that the minister could speak to him. The reason for the discipline was not given.[44] Faithfulness to the communion service was a matter of supreme importance—so much so that two deacons would be posted at the door at the close of the service to see if any members left before the communion. If they did so, they would forfeit their membership.[45]

Caersalem was an independent congregation, responsible for the election of its officers. It was made clear that those who had been deacons in other causes but now attended Caersalem were to be regarded not as officers but as fellow members of the congregation.[46] Caersalem was a Baptist church, and in their relationships with other churches this characteristic was carefully safeguarded. If a member wished to leave Caersalem, he or she had to give assurance that they were not simply leaving, but intending to worship at another church. Should that church practise open communion, the departing members would not receive a recommendatory letter, even though the church might be of Baptist persuasion.[47] Such a practice tended to divide the

Baptist churches. Yet when it came to supporting their own men in the public life of the town they were united. The Baptist Union of Llanelli and District agreed a resolution that in the forthcoming local elections they would vote for the candidate who was a Baptist. The other denominations should support their own men.[48]

A number of different meetings were convened at Caersalem: on Sundays, two services and a Sunday school; a regular weekly prayer meeting; a missionary meeting on the first Monday of the month, and a further meeting on Fridays. Caersalem members also looked forward to occasional functions, such as an Easter Monday Tea Party, visits from various lecturers, and the performance of cantatas like *David the Shepherd Boy*.[49] Conscious of the need for teaching, RB formed a young people's class to study Dr Angus's *Handbook on Christian Doctrine* (translated into Welsh by RB himself, according to Brynmor P. Jones). This book was to be used again by the pastor later in his ministry.[50]

Caersalem was situated in a working-class area, and great care had to be taken with the finances. A collection was taken during the monthly communion service, but on one occasion at least it was delayed a further week to ensure that most of the members had received their wages before the Communion Sunday. The church made provision for the needs of the poor, and for many years there was the debt to clear on the building.[51]

Calls from the Rhondda

In the opinion of one of his sons, R. B. Jones's ministry in Llanelli was an 'unmixed success'.[52] He could have remained there for an extended period had he wished, but during 1899 he received two calls from the Rhondda Valley. The first of these was a unanimous call from Seion

Chapel, Porth. The details of the call had been delegated to the deacons, but they were authorised to declare that the salary would not be under £11 a month. Two of the deacons were willing to travel to Llanelli to discuss matters further with RB.[53] However, he had also heard that Salem, another chapel in Porth, was interested in him, and he therefore wrote to the Rev. Dan Davies, who was about to terminate his pastorate there.

In his reply Dan Davies was rather critical of Seion. It was a church with about 200 members, meeting in a rather small building. There was too much timber in the building, and this resulted in much perspiration when preaching there. Speaking generally, it was the older members of Salem that had left to form the cause at Seion, leaving the younger members behind at Salem. The greatest problem, however, was the lack of love between the church members at Seion.[54] Dan Davies might have been painting a true picture of the situation, but he was also clearly discouraging RB from accepting Seion's invitation to be their minister.

In contrast, when writing of the church at Salem, Dan Davies was highly commendatory: there were 400 members, a Sunday school of between 350 and 370, well-attended prayer meetings, and the minister was paid £170 per annum. Among the church members were some of the richest men in the Rhondda. Such a church appealed to RB; in his opinion it 'was the best in the country'.[55]

As a result R. B. Jones refused the call from Seion but accepted the one he received from Salem on 9 July 1899.[56] He informed his parents that the call had arrived, and they responded with pride in their son, with thankfulness to God, and with a word of warning. They rejoiced that he had been called 'to a church of such high standard & distinguished position', but the important consideration was to ensure that this was the will of God. If there was any doubt at all, then their son should 'not have the slightest hesitation in declining the invitation'.[57] RB was convinced that it was right for him to go to Salem.

The call from Salem invited him to care for the church and to 'bring many souls to Christ in this populous place'.[58] His salary, as mentioned, was to be £170 p.a., with eight free Sundays, but he was expected to be at home on Communion Sundays. On 3 October 1899, a farewell meeting was held at Caersalem, Llanelli, chaired by Dr Rowlands, Moriah, when many of the Caersalem deacons spoke highly of R. B. Jones's ministry. He received a testimonial from the church, and Mrs Jones a Bible from the Sunday school. His fellow ministers at Llanelli presented him with an album.

2
Salem, Porth,
and the dawn of revival

It was a great encouragement for RB to follow Dan Davies at Salem. The latter had worked diligently, over a period of nine years, as a careful pastor and an outward-looking leader. During his ministry, members of Salem had formed the core of new causes at Pisgah in Cymer and at Seion in Porth. Dan Davies was also concerned for the masses outside the church and had organised open-air services in the area.[1] Many people had moved into the Porth district, resulting in increased housing and sanitary problems. There was a marked increase in population between 1901 and 1911. In this period the Rhondda Valley experienced an influx of 40,000 people. They came to a Welsh-speaking mining valley that was rapidly being Anglicised. In 1901, nearly 12,000 inhabitants of the valley were monoglot Welsh speakers, but by 1911 that figure had been halved.[2]

Early days at Salem
Brought up in a working-class home himself, RB would have understood conditions in the Rhondda. The black-faced colliers and the poisonous chimneys were familiar to him. He was also aware of the tensions between workers and bosses, and of the colourful life surrounding him on all sides. While some were training greyhounds, others would be conducting choirs. One could watch a fight at a boxing booth or enjoy a cantata being performed. Socialist orators had to compete with giants of the pulpit. It would have

been impossible to ignore the religious activity of the valley, and RB had been well prepared for such activities during his stay in Llanelli. One author has claimed of this period: 'Nowhere in Great Britain is there to be found, within a similar radius, such a hive of religious enterprise as in the Rhondda Valley.'[3] In many of the chapels it would have been difficult to find a free evening with no meeting arranged.

A welcome meeting was held for RB, at which Ceinfryn Thomas, Dowlais, and Charles Davies, Cardiff, were the preachers. The new pastor settled down quickly. As an aspiring Nonconformist minister he was on good terms with the wealthier members in the church, and was fortunate to have the support of William Evans, JP, a deacon of the church and an influential person in the Rhondda.[4]

RB's tremendous energy was soon evident. At the time of his arrival the chapel building was in good condition, electric light had been installed and all debt cleared. The pastor ministered to the whole church but made special efforts to meet the needs of the young people. He believed that the introduction of music—classical music especially—would appeal to them and create an interest. He laid great stress on the instruction of the church. The younger children were taught with the aid of a magic lantern (an early form of projector), while the older ones were introduced to Dr Angus's *Handbook* and to the *Hyfforddwr Salem* ('The Salem Instructor'), an occasional booklet edited during its two years' existence by RB himself. Another means of feeding the people was by lectures on such topics as 'Oliver Cromwell', 'Vavasor Powell', 'John Bunyan' and 'The Waldensians'.[5] Many churches invited him to give lectures, and his 'Wanted! Another Elijah or Luther for the next Protestant Reformation' made him popular in many areas.[6]

As a Baptist, RB was committed to the local Baptist Ministers Association and to the Baptist Union of England and Wales. On one occasion, when the Union made an appeal on behalf of missions, RB sat in the church vestry waiting for members to come with their contributions. The eventual sum collected was £300. When the Union urged churches to hold prayer meetings for revival, RB responded willingly, and during one short period thirty-two conversions were recorded at Salem.[7] The pastor was also always ready to help other causes in the valley. The English Baptist cause in Cwm-parc, for example, was indebted to him: 'One outstanding minister was the Rev. R. B. Jones, who regularly came once a month and who would not allow us to pay even his expenses.'[8]

This outward success, however, was not a true indication of R. B. Jones's spiritual state. On those early days in Salem Brynmor Pierce Jones commented:

> All things considered the way seemed open for a gradual development as an active, energetic pastor and organiser, fitting quite easily into the general pattern of religious life. He preached earnestly and evangelically, prayed much, worked hard; but there was no stirring of the spirit yet; he was not yet touched with the live coal from the altar.[9]

This agrees with RB's assessment of himself at this time:

> Beneath a seemingly disdainful indifference a hunger was being created which presently would become intolerable. In the providence of God, early in 1903, they found themselves fairly near neighbours. Seriously minded by this time, and having discovered affinity one with the other, they began meeting for prayer, and other forms of spiritual intercourse.[10]

The immediate context of this quotation shows that RB was referring to himself and W. S. Jones. It is strange that he mentions 1903, as W. S. Jones did not move to the Rhondda until early in 1904. The quotation is, however, a clear expression of RB's spiritual need, and of the close relationship that developed between himself and W. S. Jones.

The personal need of Salem's minister was closely related to the need of the country in general. As mentioned earlier, RB attended prayer meetings for revival; he also attended the meeting of a group of Baptist ministers who began praying for revival in 1902. Such was the interest in this meeting that when the number grew to thirty-five it had to be divided into four groups. The ministers would share their experiences with their respective congregations and this helped raise an awareness of the spiritual needs of Wales and of the needs of their own areas in particular.[11] Many of the ministers, including RB, found the answer to their longings at Llandrindod in 1903, the venue of the first Keswick-in-Wales conference.

Llandrindod, 1903

D. Wynne Evans, a Congregational minister from Chester who had ministered in Llanelli at the same time as RB, had been to the Keswick Conference in 1894.[12] In 1896 he invited J. Rhys Davies of Aberafan, Port Talbot, to accompany him. They knew each other well, as both of them travelled throughout Wales as representatives of the Christian Endeavour movement. At Keswick they met another Welshman, the Rev. Thomas Stephens, a minister in England at the time. The three men had a burden for commencing Keswick-style meetings in Wales. A group of thirteen or fourteen like-minded men met together and shared their concerns for Wales. J. Rhys Davies returned to Keswick in 1900 and in 1901. D. Wynne Evans was again present with him in 1902. As they were walking together D. Wynne Evans turned suddenly to his friend and said, 'This Convention has to go to Llandrindod next year, in August.'[13] (August was the popular holiday period.)

The two of them went to see Mrs Jessie Penn-Lewis, a Welshwoman and one of the leaders of the Keswick movement, and she volunteered to speak to Albert Head, the chairman of the Keswick Convention. The latter responded positively to the suggestion of having a Keswick-in-Wales and suggested that H. D. Phillips, Llandrindod, act as secretary, and Arthur Morgan, Llandrindod, as treasurer.[14] F. B. Meyer had visited Llandrindod in 1902, speaking at meetings arranged by H. D. Phillips, and this was a great help in furthering the necessary arrangements.[15] J. Rhys Davies corresponded with H. D. Phillips and Mrs Penn-Lewis and these two gained support from many, including Dean Howell of St. Davids, for the venture.[16] J. Rhys Davies and O. M. Owen were appointed as general secretaries. O. M. Owen, a minister at Penydarren, was another who, like RB, was seeking a deeper experience of God.

Slowly, RB was brought into contact with these Keswick organisers. He had been restless in spirit since the Llanelli period, when he first came under the influence of W. S. Jones. The latter had returned from America, where he had received a profound experience of God. As noted, he came to know RB on his return, when he ministered at Carmarthen and before RB left Llanelli for Salem. W. S. Jones described his friend at this time: 'I found that he was capable of serious thought concerning the real hidden condition of one's soul.'[17] A further experience during these months that greatly affected R. B. Jones was the death of his wife Lizzie in 1901. They had been married for only six years and the bereavement intensified his spiritual longings.

He and W. S. Jones corresponded with one another. W. S. Jones revealed his thoughts to his friend:

There are indications of the Spirit moving. It gladdens one's heart to find here and there brethren burdened with the desire to gain higher levels in the Christian life than those trodden by ordinary Christians.[18]

And RB wrote to O. M. Owen, expressing his own feelings:

O, is there not a need for us to be filled with the Spirit? I believe that there is a tide in God's wise providence, and if we are caught in its flood we will be carried on to great success in our work.[19]

This letter to O. M. Owen was dated 15 April 1903, and a direct result of it was the arranging of a meeting at Frondeg on the second Tuesday of May, during which RB, Cynog Williams and O. M. Owen opened their hearts to one another.[20] They knew of the Keswick Conference but at that time were not aware of the arrangements for Keswick-in-Wales at Llandrindod. They knew also that F. B. Meyer had ministered at Llandrindod, and they therefore decided to invite him to the Rhondda. In the event, he could not come, but he told them of the intended convention at Llandrindod in August. 'The letter from Dr. Meyer was the first intimation the young ministers referred to received of the proposed first Llandrindod Wells Convention.'[21] RB invited other ministers to attend the convention and arranged lodgings for them. These included the Baptist ministers W. S. Jones, O. M. Owen (Penydarren), Cynog Williams (Aberdare), R. S. Morris (Cwmafan), James Nicholas (Tonypandy), Mendus Williams (Pont-y-gwaith) and Gwynhefin Thomas (Cwm-parc, Treorci).[22]

The main speakers at Llandrindod were Evan Hopkins of Holy Trinity Church, Richmond, London (one who had been a strong influence on Jessie Penn-Lewis), Charles Inwood, J. S. Holden and F. B. Meyer.[23] The burden of the messages was one of consecration. Three steps should be taken to realise that goal:

    1. Confession of sin.
    2. Identification with Christ.
    3. Receiving of the Holy Spirit.[24]

As well as the main meetings, other significant events occurred. A group that included RB and O. M. Owen were chatting together, when suddenly O. M. Owen turned to RB and said that he could not smoke any more. RB decided to stop smoking as well. On another occasion RB had a personal interview with F. B. Meyer, who urged him to receive the Spirit rather than be guilty, like the Jews whom Paul rebuked, of waiting for a sign.[25]

Many ministers passed through the gates of a deeper spiritual experience during that first week in August 1903. The change was profound: 'A heavenly dawn broke on the souls of some of us'; 'A new world opened up for me'; they had 'crossed the Rubicon'.[26] A few weeks later RB described his own experience:

> Oh how sweet it is to pray. And what a wonderful book the Bible has become. Formerly it was a collection of texts; now its every word is fraught with a message for me personally. And is not the greater wonder reviewed, when one thinks, that he was content for so long, to live without it. And how grandly simple it is, Jesus Christ living in me.[27]

RB made another reference to this first Keswick-in-Wales Convention twenty years later:

> Twenty years ago I was at my first convention. God spoke through one speaker's message on the text 'Present

your bodies a living sacrifice'. It was that morning for the first time in my life I realised the word was actually 'bodies'. I realised that God demanded my body.[28]

The body had troubled him, but now he knew that he could gain the victory over its desires.

At home in Salem, his people knew that something had happened to RB. There was a new power in his preaching and a greater desire to seek those outside the church and outside of Christ. More prominence was given to prayer and evangelism. On a Saturday night he would lead others out to the streets, visiting public houses and distributing tracts. Invitations were handed out asking people to attend the 11 o'clock meeting at Salem.[29] This was the first impact of the Llandrindod Convention on the people of Salem, but the impact on RB himself was the creation of a desire within him to take the gospel to the whole of Wales. That he was to be able to do so was due to a large extent to the support he received from his second wife Catherine. She was first cousin to his first wife, and was deeply involved in RB's ministry for the remainder of his life.

Preaching tours
The experiences at Llandrindod had given RB a new awareness of the holiness of God.

> Strikingly enough, without the least collusion, and, indicative of the leading and unity of the Spirit, several young ministers found themselves preaching from the same Scripture: Isaiah's vision of the Holy, Holy, Holy God, and his call to solemn service.[30]

It was this awareness of God, the power of the Holy Spirit and the reality of the living Christ that thrust RB into his preaching tours.

RB describes his first preaching tour himself, but without mentioning the name of the preacher or the location. He refers only to a 'young and inexperienced missioner':

> Every succeeding meeting fastened still more surely the Spirit's grip on the hearts of the gathered ones. The young members of the church were specially moved. Let it be remembered that the message and its appeal were almost exclusively to those within the church. The call was to holiness. After a few nights, the 'after-meeting' method was adopted. Those desiring definite blessing were urged to remain after those who had to leave had gone. A surprising large proportion of the congregation would stay.[31]

A number of places were visited: Pen-coed, Llwynypia, Dowlais, Penydarren, Cwm-bach and Cwmafan in south Wales, and Cefn-mawr in north Wales.[32] At Cwm-bach, Emlyn Davies (Cefn-mawr, Denbighshire) assisted the missioner, and he, together with his brother Arthur, were to take a prominent part in future revival meetings.[33] On the Saturday at Cwm-bach a young people's meeting was held, and also a meeting for church members. The meetings on the Sunday attracted large crowds, and four future missionaries dedicated their lives wholly to God. The preacher gave his remuneration for preaching to the Society for the Distribution of Spurgeon's Sermons.[34] RB was establishing a pattern for future services: he was making preaching central; he was concentrating initially on church members; he gave attention particularly to the young people; and he was happy to have a soloist singer assisting in the ministry.

W. S. Jones moved to Ynys-hir, Rhondda, in March 1904. It was now possible for the two friends, W. S. Jones and RB, to meet regularly for prayer and discussion, and also to

arrange preaching meetings. Both were determined to continue evangelistic work, whatever the opposition. There
were criticisms of RB in the local paper at this time, so he
was glad of W. S. Jones's company, just as the minister of
Ynys-hir was to be glad of RB's support a little later, when
trouble arose at Jerusalem, Ynys-hir.[35]

RB prepared an advertising sheet for a series of meetings to be held from Monday to Friday, 9-13 May 1904.
The two friends, together with neighbouring ministers,
were to give addresses on 'The Spiritual Life'. The services had an impact on many people from different
churches. Before the end of the series a number of
Christians took to the streets on the Saturday night inviting
people to the services the following day.[36] W. S. Jones
recalled aspects of these meetings:

> RB and his father, I was given to understand, spent
> each morning of that week turning over the leaves of
> the Bible, and devouring the Word, on questions dealt
> with the previous evening—a practice which must have
> told immensely upon the inward man. Several came to
> the classroom each night for consecration; and many an
> interesting story of that week and the work God did,
> had he to tell afterwards. On Friday night, he got up to
> declare to all present, representatives of the church life
> of Porth, his 'position and faith'. He declared, with
> great simplicity, Jesus as Lord, that he had dedicated
> himself wholly to His service, and that he received the
> Holy Ghost, whom God giveth to those who ask Him.[37]

RB repeated this statement in an after-meeting the following Saturday evening.

Two singers assisted RB in these meetings: Emlyn
Davies, who had taken part in the Cwm-bach meetings,

and Conwil Evans, from W. S. Jones's old church in Penuel, Carmarthen. One remarkable service occurred when RB preached on 'And the floods came' (Matthew 7:25).[38] Many were humbled and sought refuge from the wrath to come, but some believed that RB had been too critical of the churches. According to W. S. Jones,

> The whole of the two Rhonddas seemed to be shaken to the depths during those two weeks, and scores had a new sense of the reality of the Saviour.[39]

Converts and existing members went back from the meetings to their respective churches and shared their experiences. Many people regarded these meetings as the beginning of revival in the Rhondda.[40] One of his sons describes the effect of these meetings on RB himself:

> It was a very fateful week for R. B. Jones and it seems as if in preparing for them and in holding them, he reached the climax of his spiritual change.[41]

Different kinds of meetings were held at Treorci for three days from Whit Sunday 1904. The Rhondda Baptists met on that Sunday for a rehearsal for the main Singing Festival meetings on the Monday.[42] On that day 1,500 people came together, eager to sing and anxious to prove that the singing of the Baptists was of a high order. Much freedom of the Spirit was experienced during the Monday. Because of a stoppage in the colliery on the Tuesday, it had been decided to hold two meetings that day. In the afternoon, Charles Davies (Cardiff) was expected to speak, but was not able to be present, and his place was taken by E. W. Davies (Ton). In the evening, RB delivered an address on holiness, 'powerful, terribly severe', but presented 'with burning zeal'.[43] He expressed the need to

34

'purify the sons of Levi', reminding the congregation that it was in the temple that Christ used the whip. These meetings on the Tuesday were described as 'a combination of a Singing Festival and a Revival'.[44] On 22 June, RB preached on the same theme of holiness at Hebron, Dowlais, his home church, and effects similar to those at Treorci resulted.[45]

As well as feeding others, RB himself needed to be fed. He depended upon personal fellowship with God and fellowship with other believers, and he also appreciated the blessing of attending the Llandrindod Convention. He was present again in the 1904 meetings. F. B. Meyer was one of the main speakers, speaking on the Christ-centred life, while A. T. Pierson spoke on the Second Coming of Christ under the following headings: return, reign, refreshing, revival, restitution, regeneration, final redemption and final reconciliation. As he spoke of the glorified state of believers, the congregation burst into praise, and the preacher led the singing of 'Crown Him Lord of all'.[46] The themes of Sonship and of the Second Coming were soon to be very prominent in RB's preaching. He also found great encouragement in a prayer meeting at which the presence of God became very real. Unknown to himself at the time, he was to need these encouragements, because July and August 1904 were to be difficult months for him.

The Call to Ainon, Ynys-hir
The deacons at Ainon, Ynys-hir (a daughter church of Salem, Porth) asked RB for permission to present his name to the church as a possible minister. He agreed to their request and on 9 July 1904 the church extended to him a call to be the minister.[47] Most men would probably have refused the invitation immediately, but RB felt that he

should consider it seriously, despite the many difficulties involved.

The two churches could hardly be compared. Salem was a strong, thriving church with a happy relationship between pastor and people. Ainon, on the other hand, was weak numerically and lacked members of substance, such as some of those at Salem. Its membership included a greater percentage of colliers than at Salem. In addition, Ainon was not a very peaceful church—many divisions had marred its witness. 'There had been bitter scenes even at the Communion Table.'[48] Indeed, RB himself had been a member of a panel sent to Ainon in an attempt to calm the waters there. There was, moreover, a substantial financial consideration. He knew that his salary at Ainon would be less than at Salem and he had a wife and young family to support. To make matters worse, when he eventually accepted Ainon's invitation, he received a letter from his members at Salem pressing him not to leave them.[49]

Nevertheless, RB did accept the invitation, and he sent the church at Ainon a long letter confirming arrangements and presenting his own suggestions for his forthcoming ministry.[50] Both parties had agreed that, in preparation for a fresh start, all the officers should resign. For a period of three to six months a committee of five would be responsible for church affairs. These were to be chosen 'by lot' and not by a vote. A suitable person attending the church, not of necessity a member, should act as secretary. No worldly means were to be used to support the church; it should not depend financially on *eisteddfodau*, concerts or parties. Members should be spiritual enough to respond willingly to the needs of the church.[51]

No one was to be accepted into membership (having received believers' baptism) without signing the temperance pledge. RB acknowledged that this could not be applied to existing members, but he expected of them and of new members that they would not frequent public houses. The prospective minister also asked for the right to nominate his successor. He believed that it would be unfortunate if, whenever he left Ainon, someone of a different mind should follow him. His last point concerned the salary. He did not specify any particular amount but asked the church to provide a manse, emphasising that the expenditure involved should not be more than £20 p.a.[52]

Many people have suggested reasons for RB's going to Ainon: he might have thought he could be freer to travel the country, or that it would be easier for him there to preach particular doctrines. But RB's son, Geraint Jones, disagreed. He believed his father was acting in accordance with God's will, and that involved in this were concerns over his health, or at least his stamina:

> Great things were in the air. He sensed this, and knew that somewhere in the strange situation God's purpose was veiled, but waiting to blaze forth. He was thirty-five years of age and his constitution had lost much of its reserve of energy in his fight with tuberculosis in earlier years.[53]

The acceptance of this call to Ainon, Ynys-hir, was 'the most important single event in the life of R. B. Jones'.[54] There is no doubt that he was walking by faith and not by sight.

R. B. Jones's new ministry was to commence at the end of November 1904, but many significant events were to occur before then, during the September and October of that year. RB had promised to visit Cefn-mawr in north Wales, and he fulfilled his appointment.[55] His friend Cynog Williams (Aberdare) had also invited him to take part in a series of meetings in October. Cynog Williams has described the background to these meetings. He had come into contact with O. M. Owen 'last Christmas' (1903) and had been to Keswick in 1903.[56] Since then he had preached the Keswick message, during his Sunday morning services especially. Towards the end of September 1904, his church held prayer meetings every night: 'The schoolroom was filled and we were compelled to hold them in the chapel.'[57] RB was being asked to confirm the work by ministering to them at the Church Anniversary Services on 24 October 1904.

RB's home church at Hebron, Dowlais, also continued to invite him to minister to them. He had been there already in March and June 1904, and was asked back again in October.[58] When he arrived, a series of prayer meetings that had started on 25 August were in their fifth week, with large numbers still attending. Ceinfryn Thomas, the minister, invited RB, R. S. Morris (Cwmafan) and W. A. Jones (Merthyr Tydfil) to join him in the ministry of the Word. The congregation was so large that they had to move from the vestry to the chapel. Ceinfryn Thomas mentioned that many who were not members were coming to faith in Christ. The church asked RB to return again for a further visit on Christmas Day of that year. The resulting revival meetings continued throughout that Christmas holiday period and well into 1905.[59]

Churches in Trecynon, Aberdare, Porth and Llwynypia were experiencing the manifest power of God's Spirit before November 1904. At Trecynon on 13 November— the day that Evan Roberts ventured out from Loughor to Aberdare—'the cloud was on the point of breaking'.[60] The message delivered by Evan Roberts down the road at Bryn Seion, Trecynon, had already been taught at Heolyfelin, Trecynon, for some months.

Another source of inspiration during this October was the visit of Dr R. A. Torrey and Charles Alexander to Cardiff. RB was aware of and particularly interested in Torrey's concern for Bible schools and for revival. RB and E. W. Davies (Ton, Rhondda) attended some of these meetings at Cardiff. They joined with others afterwards at the free meal provided by the Cory brothers.[61] Geraint Jones was of the opinion that it was this Cardiff crusade that really drove his father to prayer.[62] It must, therefore, have moved him to remarkable lengths and diligence, for prayer had been of vital importance to RB long before this. He admired the work of evangelists like Torrey and Alexander:

> So deeply was he impressed by the method of evangelism that he would have converted our chapels to Mission Halls, if he followed his own impulses, so as to get the people out of their ruts. He conducted a mission in the church of one of our mutual friends, and had a platform built over the pulpit with a view of breaking down conventionalism.[63]

The time for the move to Ainon was fast approaching, but in the meantime there was one more preaching tour to which he had committed himself. RB had promised to go to Rhosllannerchrugog.

Rhosllannerchrugog

RB had been to Cefn-mawr, near Wrexham, in April 1904, and had been asked to return in September. Members from Penuel Baptist Church, Rhosllannerchrugog, were present at the September meetings and were so impressed with the preaching that they invited RB to Rhos in November 1904. He agreed to spend the period 8-18 November in the town, or rather, in 'the largest village in Wales', as Rhos was known.

A number of events had prepared the way for RB. The evangelist Rosina Davies had preached at Capel Mawr Chapel (Calvinistic Methodist, Rhos)—'all churches joining, the chapel though so large, was overcrowded each night'.[64] The annual meetings at Seion, Ponciau, on 19-20 July, were blessed in a remarkable way, when Thomas Shankland (Bangor) and J. R. Jones (Pontypridd) were the guest preachers. Thomas Shankland preached on Ephesians 3, and J. R. Jones on 'The impossibility of believers in Christ being lost' and on Isaiah 55:11-12. He repeated the invitation '*Dere mewn*' ('Come in'), and there were loud amens from the congregation.[65] Many of those present were reminded of the 1859 Revival. The ministry of these two men at Ponciau was followed by a visit of the Rev. Charles Davies (Cardiff).[66]

The suggestion to invite RB to Rhos had come from the Rev. Evan Williams, minister of Penuel, and it was at his home that RB stayed during his visit.[67] It is also worth noting that when RB was ministering in Rhos, O. M. Owen was leading a series of meetings at Rhymney.

> I was conducting a week's mission in the Rhymney Valley that same week, and we exchanged letters twice that week, for we were privileged to see some of the wonderful work of God. The heavens were rent and the mountains began to flow down at His presence. Verily, Pentecost was with us, and that which was spoken of by the prophet Joel was again fulfilled.[68]

The people of Rhymney and of Rhos, as well as those of Loughor, were together receiving experiences that led them inevitably to make comparisons with the prophecies of Joel and with the extraordinary events of Pentecost.

The events of this series of meetings at which R. B. Jones preached during his eleven days at Rhos may be summarised as follows:[69]

Tuesday

A disappointing congregation. A powerful sermon aimed at quickening the churches. The burden of the sermon was 'a vision of God—the chief need of the churches', based on Isaiah's vision. No after-meeting was held because the message was for the church.

Wednesday

A better congregation and a better meeting. The message, as on the previous evening, dealt with the holiness of God. Many felt the truth to be piercing and timely.

Thursday

A much larger congregation. The sermon was on 'The Kingship of Christ'. The emphasis was on total commit-ment—the impossibility of serving two masters. Many were convicted of their shortcomings. After the sermon, the preacher urged the congregation to take part in prayer, give a word of testimony or sing. Many responded to his appeal. On reflection, many at Rhos believed that this was the most influential meeting of the series.

Friday

The chapel was overcrowded. It was a night never to be forgotten. Once again the message of Isaiah, 'Woe unto me', gripped the congregation. In the two-hour-long after-meeting many confessed their coldness in God's work. RB made appropriate remarks after each contribution. The meeting closed just before 10.30 p.m.

Saturday

RB went with the Rev. Evan Williams to Liverpool to hear Dr Torrey. The first meeting was a Bible-reading, a type of meeting that RB believed would be of benefit to the people of Wales. In the evening, Dr Torrey delivered a powerful sermon.

Sunday (*13 November, the day on which Evan Roberts arrived at Trecynon, Aberdare*)
In the morning RB preached to a full chapel on John 15:10. In the afternoon the young people came together for a prayer meeting. RB read a portion from the Book of Joshua. He referred to his own experience 'fifteen months ago', when he committed himself fully to God. He made an appeal for consecration and many hands were raised in response. In the evening RB preached on 2 Corinthians 5:14-15. The spirit of revival fell on many churches in Rhos during this day.

Monday
After the afternoon prayer meeting in Penuel, RB led a procession from the Square through Mountain Street to School Street, where a brief service was held. One meeting took place between two public houses, 'the gates of hell', according to the preacher. He declared that Christ would bring no one from hell, but that he was able to save from the gates of hell. RB's message in the evening was based on 1 Peter 1:18-19. Eight persons remained behind.

Tuesday
Two stayed behind after the afternoon prayer meeting. RB's text in the evening was Romans 3:22-27. There was a good hearing and a further two people stayed behind.

Wednesday
The afternoon women's prayer meeting set the congregation on fire. RB gave a brief address. The chapel was comfortably full in the evening when the preacher's message was Matthew 13:3-8. Nine stayed behind.

Thursday
One person stayed behind after the afternoon service. Later in the afternoon RB attended the ministers' fraternal, where a decision was made to study A. B. Davidson's *Theology of the Old Testament*. (This is a sad indication of the very mixed nature of the theology of Welsh ministers at the time. A. B. Davidson was a pioneer in this country of those introducing rationalistic elements into Old Testament studies.) Penuel was crowded for the evening service, many failing to get admittance. RB preached a powerful sermon on Genesis 7:10. Twelve people stayed behind.

Friday
Prayer meetings were held throughout the day. Worshippers would leave to find something to eat and then return as quickly as possible. In the meetings, many would pray at the same time. The President's chair was left empty all day, as an acknowledgement that the real leader was the Holy Spirit. Seven people professed conversion. In the evening, O. J. Owen read from John, chapter 3. RB's text was 1 Timothy 1:15, and twenty-one people responded to the call of the gospel. The vestry was turned into an inquiry room and RB summarised the message that he had given in the chapel. David Ellis and William Jones were the soloists. (E. K. Jones, a cousin of RB, was present at this meeting.)

At the close of the series of meetings, the church officers met with RB to receive his suggestion as to how to continue and confirm the awakening that they had experienced. It is unfortunate that these suggestions were never put in print. On Saturday morning Evan Williams took RB to the station, and then returned to a meeting being held at Penuel.[70]

The Spirit of God continued his work at Penuel and at Rhos long after RB had left. The awakening was characterised by intensity of prayer, by regular preaching, by processions and by an emphasis on social work. RB returned to south Wales and to his new pastorate at Ainon, Ynys-hir.

3
November 1904 to December 1906

On 20 November 1904, RB commenced his ministry at Ainon. The church was unusually full but, for reasons mentioned previously, the 'sedd fawr'—the 'big seat' for the deacons and officers—was empty. This was one aspect of the steps taken in preparation for a fresh start at Ainon.

November to December 1904
In the Rhondda Valley generally, circumstances were favourable for the spread of the gospel. Other evangelists were holding meetings in the region, as well as RB and W. S. Jones. Frank Weaver, a converted collier, was active, and Richard Cory, the Cardiff philanthropist, had presided over one of the meetings as an expression of his willingness to support evangelists in south Wales.[1]

The Rhondda also welcomed James Oatey from the East End of London, and he made his base at Ainon.[2] He had intended to visit for a week, but such were the encouragements that he remained a further week. The local paper followed events closely. Within a few days there was 'an indefinable influence in the very atmosphere'.

Each night a service in the chapel was preceded by several short open-air services at different points of vantage. Mr Oatey is a remarkable open-air preacher, and wonderfully gifted for such work. Possessing a strong physical constitution, a striking appearance, a voice like a trumpet, genial manners and wonderful tact, he soon gathers around him a large crowd, to whom he commends the Saviour in a most effective manner.[3]

One such meeting was held in the Cymer Colliery Yard, when thousands listened to an hour-long sermon. A good number returned to Salem vestry to a second meeting that continued until 11 p.m. Another open-air service was held in Hannah Street, where James Oatey made use of Salem's steps as a pulpit.

Open-air meetings were useful for preaching the gospel and also for advertising the evening services. In the chapel in the evening, James Oatey would give a brief address and then appeal for response.[4] As his meetings proceeded, there was a marked increase in the numbers responding. On Saturday 3 December, as many as 74 inquirers went into the vestry. The missioner also gave two lectures. One was on 'Billy Bray' and the other was entitled 'Six Years Among Thieves at Whitechapel'.[5] This was something rare in the context of revival. The thrilling aspects of the East End ministry appealed to the congregation and, as most of them came from a religious background, they sympathised with the nature of the work James Oatey was doing in London.

A week of meetings had been held before the more famous visit of Evan Roberts to Porth on 27 November. He visited a number of churches in the area, including Salem, but does not seem to have spoken at Ainon, Ynys-hir. The meeting at Salem was announced for 7.30 p.m., but the people had started to gather by mid-afternoon and, at the time the meeting commenced, hundreds were standing outside the chapel. At another meeting, Evan Roberts spoke for an hour. His main emphasis during the visit was on the love of God and on forgiveness.[6]

RB continued to minister occasionally at Salem. He preached powerfully there at a baptismal service, when twenty-six persons were being baptised. After the baptism, many took part in prayer; Mrs Morris, the wife of the Baptist minister at Cwmafan, gave a brief address, and the children present were also spoken to. It was said of the meeting that 'the excitement was high, but controllable'.[7] At Noddfa, Pont-y-gwaith, RB baptised nine persons. He asked each one in turn if they believed on the Lord Jesus Christ, and each of them replied positively and whole-heartedly.[8] It is also known that he visited Cwmafan during December 1904. From the last week of November to the end of December, RB had spent a considerable time ministering away from home. Early in January 1905 he again left on his travels, and this time he was bound for north Wales.

Anglesey

RB went to Anglesey at the invitation of the Holyhead Free Church Council. Two pastors, David Lloyd and David Hopkin, had heard RB preach at a Baptist Festival and had been much impressed. There were tokens of spiritual quickening upon his ministry and this had created a desire in them for a spiritual awakening on the island. The ministers had heard also of the revival in south Wales. They therefore decided to visit Morriston at a time when Evan Roberts was ministering at the Tabernacle there. They tried to obtain an interview with Evan Roberts in order to invite him to Anglesey, but he was not receiving visitors that day. The two ministers then agreed to invite RB to the island. He was glad to accept.[9] Prayer meetings were held in preparation for his visit. He arrived on 3 January 1905, and David Lloyd met him at the station and took him to the manse. Before leaving for the evening service, they prayed together, claiming 'the promise of the Father'.[10] RB himself described this first meeting:

At 8 p.m. I went to the chapel. A prayer meeting was already in progress, and soon the chapel was filled to the doors. Many had to stand for lack of sitting accommodation; the singing was not at all good; very slow & lacking in fire and spirit. The place seemed pervaded with an air of curiosity. Many were there for the purpose of witnessing unusual sights; at least, so it seemed to me. After a season of silent prayer I spoke on the Baptism of the Spirit attempting to show its distinctiveness from the initial stages of spiritual life; and emphasizing surrender to King Jesus as the one essential condition.[11]

About twelve people responded to the call to consecration and one person professed conversion.

On the afternoon of 4 January, the ladies came together for prayer. The schoolroom was full but there was a reluctance to take part in prayer. After a strong exhortation from the preacher, about six ladies prayed and one gave her personal testimony. In the evening, RB spoke to an attentive congregation on the holiness of God. Many in the congregation were deeply moved, and convicted of the low state of their spiritual lives. Conscious that the Spirit of God was at work, RB 'purposely curtailed the service, being anxious that the people should go home alone to settle their differences silently with God'.[12] It is worth noting that services were not always prolonged during the Revival—there were also times when they were curtailed. An open-air service was held after the chapel meeting. During the week such meetings were held regularly, especially at the Old Station, with the local ministers taking a prominent part.[13] A ready helper was the soloist, Arthur Davies.[14]

Much fervour characterised the ladies' afternoon meeting of 5 January. More women took part and there was a strong emphasis on intercession for particular individuals. The theme of the evening message was 'The Kingship of Christ' and was based on Romans 14:9. Those present were impressed by the testimony of a bicycle dealer, who vowed that he would never again sell bicycles on a Sunday—an interesting example of the impact of the Revival on Sunday observance. This meeting commenced at 8 p.m. and finished three hours later. Numbers increased for the afternoon meeting of 6 January and it had to be moved from the vestry to the chapel, as had occurred earlier in meetings at Trecynon and Hebron, Dowlais. Much power was felt in the evening service, in which RB spoke on the fullness of salvation through the Spirit.[15]

The men joined the women for the afternoon meeting of 7 January. The floor of the chapel was full and included many from the surrounding countryside. At the close of the service, RB called for a meeting of young people:

> In the afternoon at three came the next meeting. This was specially intended for young people. Romans 12.1 was the text and the Spirit worked while I urged them to full dedication of themselves to the glory of Jesus. It was inspiring to hear at the close 'Yes, Lord' come from the lips of a large number.[16]

Several requests for prayer were made in the evening service. One lady prayed for her unconverted husband, and a few moments later the husband came forward acknowledging Christ as Saviour.

RB described the morning meeting of 8 January as a time of refreshing from the presence of the Lord. Two people professed conversion and the whole congregation stood in an act of consecration. In the evening meeting he exhorted the people to be fruit-bearing Christians. Only about 25 were present at the beginning of a morning prayer meeting on 9 January, but others arrived later. The preacher had no doubt that it was 'easily an upper chamber service'.[17] RB rested in the afternoon, and in the evening service his subject was 'Confessing Christ'. He was truly grateful for what had happened during the week:

> Many have realized their Pentecost. It is a totally new church. God has worked wonders in the one week and will do greater things through these people. To Him be the glory for ever.[18]

During this first week of R. B. Jones's ministry in Anglesey, 75 persons had professed conversion or had consecrated themselves anew to God.[19] RB himself reflected on this period:

> It is of course quite impossible to adequately conceive of, not to speak of describing, a work which reaches deep and wide into the lives of the people. They are exulting in new discoveries of what is their inheritance in the Salvation wrought for them and in them by the Lord Jesus, and, best of all, the pastor has been led to a crucifixion of self, in order that the life of Christ might be made manifest in and through him. He seems mastered by the Spirit, and his witness before his own people was most inspiring.[20]

He acknowledged, however, that an even greater manifestation of the Spirit was needed, because, in some cases, 'the characters of the officers are notoriously bad', and he added, 'The Winnower is needed here!'[21]

On Thursday afternoon, 12 January, RB preached at Mount Pleasant English Baptist Church, before moving on to Llanfachreth.[22] The minister and some of the people had been present at the Holyhead meetings, and had been impressed not only by the preaching, but also by the care given to those that professed conversion. After returning home there were discussions in the village generally regarding the revival meetings. On Sunday morning, 15 January, the Baptist minister shared his experiences with the congregation. As he was doing so a man called William Jones cried out, praising God for mercy on the past forty years of his life. A sense of awe came over the whole congregation.[23]

In the afternoon the same minister shared his experience with his people at Llanddeusant. His comment, 'We should have been in Gethsemane sweating blood', touched every heart. RB preached at Llanfachreth that evening. Once again the theme was the holiness of God. The meeting was left open for people to take part, and there was much rejoicing. It seemed as if everyone in the 600-strong congregation had contributed.[24] During the Young People's Meeting on the following Tuesday, RB exhorted them to live a life of consecration, and condemned habits that were to be avoided, in particular the reading of novels. According to the preacher, this habit arose from a craving after excitement. When RB visited Rhyd-wyn, he asked them to confess their sins—present sins, not those of the past. The congregation wept quietly. During these few days, 70 converts were recorded at Llanfachreth.[25]

The missioner commenced his ministry at Llannerch-y-medd on 18 January. Students from the Theological Colleges in Bangor knew that he was in Anglesey, and a group of them, mainly from the Baptist College, journeyed by train to meet him. At Gaerwen they met David Lloyd, Holyhead, and travelled with him to Llannerch-y-medd, stopping mid-journey at Llangefni, where they held a meeting in the market-square. May John, one of the Revival's soloists, joined them. The gospel witnesses made use of a fountain ledge as a pulpit and a large crowd gathered to listen to them. May John stayed in Llangefni, but David Lloyd and the students went on to Llannerch-y-medd.[26]

RB was glad to see the students, and one of them related that at Llannerch-y-medd,

> David Lloyd ushered us into a shop where the Rev. R. B. Jones was sitting all alone in the middle room: 'Hallelujah!' he cried, 'The Lord has answered prayer. I have been asking him to give me some helpers.' In next to no time the people of Llannerch-y-medd had found lodgings for us; two of us stayed with Mr and Mrs Sturdy, the parents of Mrs Tecwyn Evans. We found ourselves staying the week without our Principal's knowledge or consent.[27]

When the Principal realised that some of his students were in revival meetings, he sent another student to bring them back to the College. But instead of retrieving the wanderers, the summoner remained also in order to help in the work of the revival.[28]

One of RB's main themes was assurance of salvation. After such a message, a well-known character in the area came forward to the front of the chapel to confess Christ as Saviour. He was *Telynor Seiriol* (Harpist Seiriol), known for his loose living and for his skill on the harp. He had performed for Edward VII when the king was welcomed at Holyhead during a royal visit to Dublin. *Telynor Seiriol* was the owner of the Golden Harp of Llanover, a trophy that he had won in a competition. His conversion proved genuine and was regarded as one of the most marvellous miracles of the Revival.[29]

The students took part in the services and were themselves deeply influenced by the Spirit of God. In one meeting,

> The Missioner, looking from the pulpit, saw a college student full length on the floor of the big pew. Suddenly the young man arose, and putting his hand in his pocket, he took out his pipe and publicly handed it to the Missioner.[30]

Others followed suit until the table in front of the chapel was covered with pipes and tobacco. RB had not mentioned smoking in his address.

As in Llanfachreth and other places, RB arranged a young people's meeting at Llannerch-y-medd:

> Two hundred came together to hear his appeal to destroy self by giving themselves wholly to Christ. Comparing the meeting with Mount Carmel where Elijah had prepared the altar, sacrifice and water but God sent the fire, he said very solemnly, 'You have been touched, you have considered, you have given yourselves to the Lord. Now I will pray that the Holy Spirit will come.' The young people knelt in rows and their Pentecost came.[31]

At the end of three days in Llannerch-y-medd, RB and the students continued on their tour and reached Amlwch.

At Amlwch RB's message was again taken from Isaiah, chapter 6. He preached three times on the Sunday, 22 January, and described the evening service:

> The light of God's holiness was turned upon the hearts of those present. Conviction of sin, and its terrible desert, was so crushing that a feeling of despair grew

over all hearts. So grievous a thing was sin; so richly and inevitably did it deserve the severest punishment of God, that hearts questioned, Could God forgive? Could he cleanse? Then came the word about the altar . . . As one man, first with a sigh of relief, and then, with a delirious shout of joy, the whole congregation sprang to its feet. The vision had completely overwhelmed them, and, one is not ashamed to tell it, for a moment they were beside themselves with joy.[32]

The place was filled with the presence of God, and the preacher withdrew. His preaching itinerary came to an end at Llangefni on 26 January. Here, though it was midday, a large congregation gathered at the Market Hall to listen to him preach.[33]

On returning to south Wales, RB preached for his friend D. S. Jones at Bridgend. In one of the meetings the Bridgend minister saw a ball of fire falling from the sky, signifying, he believed, that God was doing his purifying work in the churches.[34] RB also found time to travel, with W. W. Lewis, to west Wales, and ministered at Aberaeron, Pontsaeson and Llan-non.[35] He was also busy organising and making arrangements for local conventions. (These will be discussed in chapter 5.) No more than a month later he was back in north Wales.

Caernarfon
Revival had broken out in Caernarfon before the end of 1904 and by the beginning of the new year had made 'substantial progress'.[36] Joint meetings between Anglicans and Nonconformists were effective means of spreading the revival and the young people especially were full of zeal, visiting the homes with invitation tickets to the meetings.[37] Immediately before RB's arrival, Joseph Jenkins had held

meetings in the town. RB had been invited to the area by the Caernarfon Free Church Council, and he was glad to accept. As at Anglesey, Arthur Davies and the students from Bangor supported the missioner.[38] Arthur Davies was the guest artist at a St David's Day celebration in Moriah. He, like other singers, was happy enough to take part in such celebrations during the revival period.

Simultaneous meetings were held at Engedi and at the Guild Hall. The chapel was crowded for the first meeting when RB delivered a 'sane and thoughtful sermon, in the course of which he deprecated loud shouting and signs of violent emotion'.[39] Meanwhile, in the Guild Hall, there were signs of violent emotion, because the students were on their knees 'as if hypnotized' and in a short time the place was like 'a boiling cauldron'.[40] Order was restored with the singing of *'Mae e'n fendigedig'* ('He is glorious').

The next evening RB again preached at Engedi and then moved to the Guild Hall to join the students. There is no doubt that his presence there contributed to the more orderly meeting that occurred that second evening. A representative of the Mission to Seamen got up to protest against keeping children out late at night. RB offered parents an opportunity to leave, and then announced a hymn, *'Duw mawr y rhyfeddodau maith'* ('Great God of wonders'), but no one moved. Arthur Davies sang a hymn *'Beth a wnei di â'r Iesu?'* ('What will you do with Jesus?'). RB asked those who believed in Jesus to stand and sing a hymn and then brought the meeting to a close at 11 p.m.[41]

The converting power of the word in the meeting on the third evening was overwhelming and many thought that they were choking. It was 'indescribable'.[42] Conscious of the strength of emotions present, RB turned to prayer, confessing Christ as Saviour and King, and his prayer brought joy to many a troubled heart.

The revivalist continued on his journey, visiting Llanberis with Arthur Davies, before moving on to Tal-y-sarn, Llanllyfni and Clynnog. There was considerable response in these places, but not as much as in Caernarfon itself. The Sunday following, by which time he had left the region, 21 were received into membership at Pendref; 46 at Caersalem; 64 at Siloh; and 36 at Salem.[43]

Further journeys in north and south Wales
After preaching at Birkenhead R. B. Jones returned to south Wales. At the end of March he was ministering at Treherbert and Rhymney.[44] Much of April was again spent in north Wales. He divided his time between Corwen, Cynwyd, Cefn-mawr and Glynceiriog. The people of Corwen were expecting 'the North Wales chief revivalist'.[45]

When RB arrived, he preached on 'Forgiveness', 'Assurance' and 'Baptism'. Emlyn Davies sang in the meetings.[46] A baptismal service was held, at which Cernyw Williams baptised four converts. As R. Tudur Jones has pointed out, baptisms had a special appeal during the Revival.[47] They were public occasions, granting opportunities for hearing public confessions of faith. A baptism in a river was an added attraction.

Cernyw Williams hoped that RB's counsel to parents would burn in the hearts of all the parents of the area. He sent his thanks to the minister of Ynys-hir for his labours at Corwen:

> Every denomination had last night additions to membership as direct results of your mission. We had a wonderful testimony meeting followed by a remarkable prayer service. I, personally, feel I have received great good. I feel very guilty for the unfruitfulness of

my past life. I am certain that had I been properly awakened I could have been of greater service.[48]

This was a typical response to RB's preaching. Many ministers were renewed and quickened in spirit. Cernyw Williams also thanked RB for the 'excellent work' he was doing to help young ministers.[49]

The first meeting at Cefn-mawr was set aside for prayer. Those present enjoyed a degree of liberty in praying, despite the fact that RB believed that there was much denominational spirit in the village. The preacher felt differently the following day, Good Friday:

> Good Friday witnessed one of the most remarkable series of meetings I have yet been privileged to attend. The crowds of people, the enthusiasm, the prayer, songs and testimonies were most remarkable. A procession of 300 or 400 had marched over from Rhos and they made the countryside ring again as they came and returned with praises of the Redeemer.[50]

Cefn-mawr and Rhos were still enjoying revival and were continuing to support the chief evangelist of north Wales.

In the morning meeting at Cefn-mawr RB spoke on 'Crucified with Christ'. Strong men were moved and 'wept like children'.[51] RB asked all who had been saved during the Revival to stand up, and many did so, unashamed of the gospel. They shared their experiences publicly and RB, as he looked upon them, knew that the name of the beast had been removed from them and been replaced by the name of the Lamb. The preacher made use of numerous Scriptures reflecting his theme: Colossians 2:14; Ephesians 2:15; Romans 6:6; Galatians 5:24, 6:14 and 2:20. In a fervent evening service his message was 'Our inheritance in Christ'.[52]

He visited five places in south Wales during the month of May and made one trip to Llandudno in north Wales. In June, he preached away at four different places in south Wales, including Dowlais,[53] before arriving at Llangollen in north Wales by the end of the month. During his mission at Llangollen, RB and his fellow revivalists experienced opposition. They had arranged a procession, and when it came to stop in order to hold a service, the local band started playing, making it impossible for RB, who was preaching at the time, to continue. Emlyn Davies, writing to Jessie Penn-Lewis, conveyed RB's opinion that the opposition was from the Devil and that the band would not prosper.[54] The missioner then moved to the town of Denbigh. In one of the meetings he spoke, as he had done in other places, to particular groupings in the congregation. He gave attention to Sunday school scholars, to parents, to deacons and to ministers, criticising failures and pointing out the duties of each group.[55]

Although not quite so busy during August, RB continued to preach and spent a week at the Llandrindod Convention. We know of two meetings that he took during September— one in Liverpool, and another in Llanelli, south Wales.

Most of RB's travels in England occurred in the years after the 1904–5 Revival but he had been to Plymouth in July and now, in September 1905, he arrived at Liverpool. He reported on some of the meetings:

Saturday, Psalm 24:7-10.
On Sunday morning I had to speak on the 'Commission of Olivet'. In the afternoon, Joshua 1:12-15, which was simply a re-emphasis of the morning's message; in the evening Philippians 2:8.

On Monday evening we had to adjourn to a large chapel. This was packed, and the message was 'Pentecost described in Acts 2', and on Tuesday evening, 'The Church that can expect Revival'.[56]

Apart from the usual themes of holiness and revival, the preacher emphasised another matter close to his heart, namely, the worldwide mission of the Church. The land of revival should send out missionaries to other countries:

God save Wales from becoming parochial in its view and sympathies.[57]

RB arrived home from Liverpool on a Monday. Everything was 'in chaos' in that he was in the middle of a move into a new house.[58] He had no time to settle down however, because before the end of the week he was away again, this time to Llanelli. At the beginning of his mission in the town he was conscious of opposition, but was confident in spirit and had, once again, the company of Arthur Davies to encourage him. The earthquake and the wind were in the ministry:

But in the small after-meetings for consecration held in the vestry, the still small voice was heard and many a soul was bent before the presence of the Lord.[59]

The preacher stayed with Trevor Jones, Bethania, and his sister, whom RB had known from the days of his ministry in the town from 1895 to 1899.

It was at the home of Trevor Jones that something unusual took place. A young girl of eighteen years of age was helping in the house. One evening, RB noticed that she was extremely agitated and when serving meals would drop things. During evening prayers, she wept and

groaned, and RB was conscious that this was not something purely physical. He believed that it was a Satanic
attack. On the last night of his stay, he, together with
Trevor Jones and his sister, prayed for the young girl, who
was present with them. In the name of Jesus they com-
manded the evil spirit to depart. It was cast out and she
jumped to her feet 'transformed with joy'.[60]

RB described the young girl's account of the experience. She had been in darkness:

> In front of her at some distance away she seemed to see
> a beautiful light falling upon an open door, whilst at her
> side in the darkness there [unclear word] be a huge
> shape doing its utmost to draw her away from the light
> and the open door. But the moment the name of Jesus
> Christ was heard, this creature let go his hold upon her
> and vanished, while she felt as if she were triumphantly
> carried towards the light and the open door.[61]

This is an example of what was a rare experience for R. B.
Jones, but it must be added to the accounts of miraculous
healings in Loughor and Penydarren, and to manifestations
of the Spirit in Bridgend and Pen-y-groes.[62]

The same pattern of itinerating may be traced in the
period from October to December, 1905. In October, for
example, there were five nights in Tredegar, south Wales,
and a tour in north Wales, when RB visited Harlech,
Pwllheli, Dolgellau and Barmouth.[63] One meeting at
Tredegar provides a good example of those occasions
when his preaching was stern. The congregation was kept
at the foot of Sinai in the presence of fire and lightning.
The message lacked the 'wooing note' that Jowett looked
for in preaching.[64] During RB's visit to Glynceiriog, north
Wales, in November, a fellow minister was conscious of

another aspect of RB's ministry. When this man entered the chapel,

> I saw his countenance shining with a heavenly radiance, and felt as if I was entering the presence of the Lord filling that place.[65]

As well as Glynceiriog, RB visited Mold, Wrexham, Rhyl and Llandudno. During the same period he preached, in south Wales, at Carmarthen, Merthyr and Trefforest.[66]

R. B. Jones never worked in partnership with Evan Roberts, but found himself sharing a meeting with him before the end of 1905. RB, Evan Roberts, Jessie Penn-Lewis and William Edwards, Principal of the Baptist College at Cardiff, were present at a meeting at Tonyrefail. Evan Roberts spoke and the Principal gave an account of the revival in Cardiff.[67] It is not known whether RB spoke or not, but having travelled to Tonyrefail, it must have been with the intention of speaking.

For RB, 1906 was a quieter year, but this did not mean that he was not often away from Ainon. The impact of the Revival was still being felt in many places. The spirit at Abercwmboi was 'bordering on the enthusiasm of the Revival',[68] and in Pen-y-groes, south Wales, 'the heavenly fire was still burning'.[69] RB visited both places, and when he travelled to Amlwch, north Wales, he found that the revival spirit was as strong there as in places in south Wales. One correspondent believed that RB's first visit to Amlwch in 1904 had made lions of them, but that his second visit had made them into lambs.[70] That is, the believers now were not only bold to witness but humble and ready to suffer for the sake of the gospel.

Occasionally meetings were arranged as a response to particular local circumstances. Towards the end of 1905, the Rev. W. S. Jones had experienced opposition as pastor of Jerusalem, Ynys-hir.[71] A small section of his congregation had turned against him because of his support for the Revival, his emphasis on open-air meetings, and his attendance at one of Pastor Howton's meetings. The ministry of the latter was one that focused on miraculous manifestations as proof of the presence of God. During the unrest, denominational committees had laboured to reconcile the chapel. RB was a member of one of these panels. Peace was achieved eventually, and the minister arranged prayer and preaching services to give thanks to God for overruling in a difficult situation. Outbursts of praise characterised these prayer meetings. RB preached in Welsh and W. S. Jones in English. In view of the circumstances, RB preached from 1 Corinthians 3:1-3 on being carnal or spiritual. He also made use of Romans 8:2 and 1 Peter 2:1-3. The soloists David Ellis and Emlyn Davies also took part in the services.[72]

Conventions

Many of the ministers of the period began to consider preaching engagements as opportunities to proclaim the message of sanctification:

> It was indeed a strange thing to see Welsh preaching festivals converted into what approximated to Holiness Conventions.[73]

The need was felt for an extended series of services concentrating on the theme of holiness: that is, to hold conventions as well as preaching services. A pattern was at hand in the form of the Llandrindod Convention. Other factors contributed to this growing movement. One was the presence in Wales of Reader Harris, QC, and another was the possible use of Free Church Councils for setting up local arrangements.

Ministers in west Wales had arranged conventions during 1903–4, and others had been held in Carmarthen, Aberdare and Cwmafan before the end of 1904. RB had taken part in the Carmarthen meetings.[74] R. S. Morris, a Welsh Baptist minister at Cwmafan, was familiar with the Llandrindod Convention and he arranged four days of Bible teaching in Cwmafan, inviting many of the prominent revival leaders to help. RB was one of those who had received invitations.[75]

Jessie Penn-Lewis was also anxious to develop convention work in Wales. She was in close touch with the main Keswick leaders: Evan Hopkins, F. B. Meyer, Charles Inwood and A. T. Pierson. She was also on friendly terms with RB and O. M. Owen. The speakers at the early conventions of 1904 had been Welshmen, but gradually English speakers were invited. This change was due mainly to Jessie Penn-Lewis.

Mrs Penn-Lewis was eager to gain the support of RB. She had heard that

> Mr Jones is a man of action and, I am told, of most balanced judgement, and with powers of a leader.[76]

After a later visit to meet RB, she commented that he was 'so intelligent and clear'.[77] She referred to him as 'a man of action' in writing to Albert Head, chairman of the Keswick Convention.[78] In his reply, Albert Head informed her that Charles Inwood had been invited to co-operate with Evan Roberts and RB in the work in Wales. These latter were exactly the two men that the Welshwoman thought capable of leading the work in Wales,[79] though she was very concerned at the effect the work would have on Evan Roberts.

A meeting was held in Cardiff in the middle of January 1905. Charles Inwood, Jessie Penn-Lewis, F. B. Meyer, Evan Hopkins, C. G. Moore, and a few Welsh ministers were present.[80] The group met for prayer at the Baptist College, where it received a welcome from Dr William Edwards. RB was in north Wales at the time, but Jessie Penn-Lewis kept him informed of what was happening. They decided to hold further meetings in Cardiff on 7-8 February. RB returned from north Wales and arranged for Charles Inwood to visit the Rhondda during his stay in the country. He was back again at the end of February, 'entering any open doors that are available'.[81]

Various meetings in February led up to the Pontypridd Convention of 15-16 March 1905. RB was responsible for the local arrangements. He appointed two local secretaries to administer the plans prepared by himself and Jessie Penn-Lewis. She believed that there was a need to bring as many people as possible together, because the Welshmen were 'deeply grounded in the letter of the Scripture' but did not know the 'experiential' possibilities of the work of the Spirit. She then made the strange comment that the main reason for this lack was the fact that the people of Wales were taken up with the Revival.[82] Her words seem to imply that a deeper experience could come to believers, not through the Revival, but through the Keswick teaching.

Albert Head presided at Pontypridd, with Charles Inwood and A. T. Pierson as main speakers. There was a suggestion that these two should speak at all the meetings, in order to avoid the problem of choosing between the various Welsh ministers. There were evident tensions involved in such a choice. On the other hand, some, including O. M. Owen, thought that speakers from Wales were being ignored. This, he believed, had been the case for the Llandrindod Convention:

> Some of the speakers that are invited are in every sense inferior to some of our Welsh brethren. If Wales is

going to be reached it must be through Welshmen. No one can touch the heart of Wales like a Welshman.[83]

These tensions re-emerged in the planning of local conventions over the next few years, and again also with the Llandrindod lists of speakers. Keri Evans, Carmarthen, did take part at Pontypridd, but his presence there did not remove completely the problematic denominational considerations of the situation. Jessie Penn-Lewis, in preparing for another convention, asked RB to find out whether the Baptist ministers were happy to invite J. M. Saunders, a Presbyterian, to the meetings.[84] RB's response is not known.

A number of ministers met at the beginning of April, convinced that 'now is the time for Convention Work'.[85] They drew up a list of possible centres: Treharris, Dowlais, Mountain Ash, Aberdare, Bridgend, Pen-coed, Llwynypia and Bargoed. RB was aware that these were places deeply affected by the Revival.

> There is an opening for the message everywhere where the revival fervour has not been ungovernable. In such places excitement must die down to a degree before there will be willing ears and hearts for the deeper things. As the process goes on there will be a need for a much larger army of workers who can teach these things.[86]

It was the need for teaching that was laid upon his heart—teaching of such a nature that those who were taught could teach others. The work would not prosper, however, without the Spirit being poured out on dry ground, as promised in Isaiah 44:3.[87]

By this time, April 1905, RB was suffering from overwork and had to cancel some appointments. O. M. Owen, for example, took his place at meetings in the Metropolitan Tabernacle in London. RB felt guilty that he should be tired in God's service. When he shared his feelings with Jessie Penn-Lewis, she rebuked him, suggesting that he 'was going ahead too fast'.[88] There was a danger that he was not listening to 'the voice' speaking to him. For all the mystical talk about 'the voice', this was wise counsel. Even during April, RB helped with arrangements for the local conventions, though O. M. Owen took most of the responsibilities. He wrote to Jessie Penn-Lewis informing her that the ministers in Wales had drawn up a list of convention speakers from Wales, but as far as the English speakers were concerned, 'we leave that to you'.[89]

There is no doubt that the visit of A. T. Pierson to Wales during June and July 1905 strengthened the convention work in Wales. He spent some time in Llwynypia, where he ministered with Charles Inwood and Keri Evans. Referring particularly to one Wednesday night service in which A. T. Pierson spoke on John 16:17, Charles Inwood said, 'I don't know that I have ever seen anything quite like the Wednesday meeting.'[90] Pearson visited Cardiff, Port Talbot, Llanelli and Carmarthen before going to Keswick in the first week in August. RB and Keri Evans were among other Welshmen at Keswick. They were taken to the 'mountain of God' in A. T. Pierson's meeting, and at one evening service that was full of praise and confession, Keri Evans saw RB taking out his gold watch-chain and placing it on the collection plate.[91]

The main Keswick leaders continued to visit Wales and, in conjunction with Jessie Penn-Lewis and some of the Welsh ministers, arranged further conventions. Cardiff became the centre for 'The South Wales Convention for the Deepening of Spiritual Life'. The first series of meetings was held in February 1906, in the Cory Hall, with John Cory providing the breakfast for the ministers.[92] Jessie Penn-Lewis drew attention to the convention in her periodical, *The Life of Faith,* and this notice must have had effect, even drawing some participants from overseas:

> Even at this first convention there were visitors from Germany and Armenia, who had read Jessie's reports and were full of expectation that the revival spirit was still there. They were not disappointed.[93]

During April 1906, RB spoke every day at Brynhyfryd, Swansea, and preached with W. S. Jones in Llwynypia.[94] He spoke for the first time at the Llandrindod Convention in August 1906. Brynmor Jones summarised the theme of the convention in one word—'daily'. Evan Hopkins spoke on 'daily deliverance', W. S. Jones on 'daily communion', and RB on 'daily rejection and crucifixion as long as the Spirit and the Blood worked in their hearts'. He reminded the congregation that 'Jesus is waiting for you to go to the Cross so that he can show you that the victory is complete and secure.' He could express a truth in a nutshell: 'There is much Cross-bearing but little crucifixion.'[95] There were difficulties at this convention. Concern was expressed regarding Evan Roberts's health and over the effect of this on his role in future developments. Jessie Penn-Lewis experienced opposition, and her breakfast talk 'caused much antagonism'. She was convinced that Evan Roberts should be kept out of convention work. As usual, she was more than ready to defend herself. Writing to RB, and addressing him as 'My dear son', she informed him that she could feel the tension at Llandrindod but was sure that it was 'the raging of hell against the Cross'.[96]

These conventions were significant for many reasons. They were the means of bringing together Christians from all denominations, and of uniting Nonconformists and Anglicans. Such unity safeguarded the aspect of fellowship in the Christian life. One of the main features of the meetings was the Bible teaching. In giving an invitation to a convention, one minister told visitors to bring a Bible and a notebook, 'because the speakers make continuous use of the scripture to support the message of the fullness of the Spirit for the whole church'.[97] Those coming were not to expect to enjoy 'an intellectual feast' or 'fleshly enjoyment', but could expect an 'encounter with the Lord'.[98] They were effective means of hammering home the twin themes of the fullness of the Spirit for believers and the Second Coming of Christ, explained in premillennial terms.

Unlike denominational meetings, female speakers were welcomed in the conventions. In Wales these included Jessie Penn-Lewis, Mrs J. M. Saunders (Swansea), Miss Mansfield, and Mrs Beresford Baker. Denominationally, 'women preachers' was a controversial matter. Some churches welcomed them, whilst others would not consider receiving them. But the conventions provided a home for them. Furthermore, they serve as a reminder of the tremendous influence that Mrs Jessie Penn-Lewis had on religious developments in Wales.

Sufficient work was undertaken during 1904–6 to ensure that the conventions would continue in the following years. RB was to be prominent in them, but he was also the minister of Ainon, and the demands of his church and his response to them need to be considered.

4
Ainon, Ynys-hir, 1904–1919

The new pastor had suggested to the church that changes should be made before he started his ministry in Ainon. Some improvements did indeed take place towards the end of 1904 and the beginning of 1905, but matters were not helped by his frequent absences at preaching engagements elsewhere.

> The lengthy absence of their pastor on some campaign, the frequent unannounced visits of evangelists at mid-week meetings and Sunday services, the arrival of scores of observers, including Europeans, who some-how expected, and got lodgings; all this was somewhat unsettling.[1]

Better progress was made during 1905. John T. Phillips was appointed assistant pastor, relieving RB of some of his burdens. Phillips was from Llanboidy, Carmarthenshire, and was one of the Baptist students that had helped RB in the revival meetings in Anglesey during January 1905.[2] He assisted for a year before leaving for Cadoxton Moors Church, but returned to the Rhondda as pastor of Bethany, Ynys-hir, from 1908 to 1921.

Ainon

A very significant meeting took place during 1905 (RB referred to it in a letter to Jessie Penn-Lewis). On her return from the Llandrindod Convention of August 1905, Catherine, RB's wife, had shared her experience there with him and with one of his sisters, and had broken down in tears. She took off the two bracelets that she was wearing, seeing them as 'superfluous ornaments'.[3] The impact of her experience affected the church also when she spoke of it during the morning service on Sunday 13 August 1905.

RB had welcomed his wife's contribution, but was convinced that some further specific action had to be taken that would help the whole church. The evening service on that Sunday was a Communion Service:

> It was laid upon my heart that there should be no administering of the Lord's Supper in our chapel again until every member was in a state of reconciliation one with the other. It was the Lord's will and it was a cross, but I took it up and trusted Him to see me through it. I put the matter plainly, and as I believe, in love before my people, urged them as they were gathered around the Cross to let their Saviour's cross slay the enmity between them, and then began the fight, and it was a terrible one. Some were broken down to the dust, whilst others became demoniacal in their wrath and anger.[4]

It was an unpleasant experience for RB, but a crucial step had been taken towards full unity, and the church was strong enough to cope with any continuing opposition from some members.

In confirming the work, RB built on the three pillars of conversion, confession and consecration. Basic to everything was his emphasis on conversion as the only way of entrance into the church. Like the other Revival leaders, RB believed that this emphasis had been neglected in the Welsh churches. Conversion should be followed by the personal confession of baptism by immersion. This, in turn, should lead to consecration. The pastor continually reminded his people of the high calling of the Christian life.

A Sunday at Ainon Chapel was a busy day. A prayer meeting was held at 9.30 a.m., followed by the morning service at 10.30. The Sunday school was at 2 p.m. An open-air service would be held at 5 p.m. during the summer months, and the evening service was at 6 o'clock.[5] The mid-week prayer meeting was well attended, as was the Bible study on Fridays during the winter. Whatever his engagements, RB would make an effort to be present at this Friday meeting. He would speak for the best part of an hour, writing his main points on a blackboard, and it was expected that these would be noted down by his hearers.[6] The meeting attracted many people from different parts of the Rhondda. For those whose interest was keenest, another similar meeting would be held on the Saturday night. He was to hold similar meetings later at Tabernacle, Porth.

Attention was also given to the children—a Children's League was formed for them.[7] They were presented with a pictorial certificate with two photographs on it, one showing the exterior and the other the interior of Ainon chapel. RB would sign each certificate. Records of attendance at the Sunday morning services were kept and marks given. There were three marks for each service: one for being present, one for punctuality, and one for reciting a verse. The children took part in a monthly Sunday morning service, and every three months a special service was held in which badges were presented to those with full marks. At the end of the year the badges were exchanged for bronze brooches. These were then further exchanged for silver and, finally, for gold brooches which were kept by the children. The young of the church were very carefully shepherded. One member, recalling these days, stated: 'The young people of those days at Ainon were to be seen in particularly every service on Sunday and in the week-night meetings.'[8]

R. B. Jones's preaching became more thematic. When preaching on a particular subject he would quote extensively from Scripture to buttress his arguments. This method proved effective, in that conversions were often recorded. As a pastor, RB did not concentrate on visiting. It was the district visitors, deacons and others who kept in touch with the members. This meant that, on the one hand, RB saw his people often at meetings, but, on the other hand, he was not close to them on a personal level. This was true even of his deacons: 'There was no familiarity to reap contempt.'[9] Some even believed that he was fanatical in his methods and preaching, but 'What we may regard as fanaticism was considered by R. B. Jones as vital to the Christian faith.'[10]

Then, in 1906, just as he was settling down in Ainon and continuing to travel the country, RB received an invitation to visit the United States of America.

America

One striking feature of the 1904–5 Revival was the way it influenced so many other countries—countries as different as France, Korea and the United States. Welsh people who had emigrated to America kept in close touch with the home country by means of correspondence, newspapers, periodicals and frequent visits. Miss Ellinor Williams, a Baptist from Llangollen, was in America on a preaching tour just before the revival started;[11] during the revival three Welshmen—J. Tudor Rees, Gwilym O. Griffith, and Dewi Michael—toured America; and then in 1906 Seth Joshua and Sam Jenkins crossed the Atlantic, and T. C. Thomas and his wife joined Sam Jenkins there later.[12]

RB accepted the invitation, and before leaving he received greetings from Evan Roberts in the form of a poem of twelve verses.[13] (Evan Roberts was always interested in

RB's work.) RB was known in America before his arrival there in 1907. In 1904 he had received a call from Hyde Park, Scranton—a church of 500 members that ran three Sunday schools.[14] Many people from the Rhondda had emigrated to America and would send reports of religious developments there to families and friends in Wales. L. Ton Evans ('Junius'), pastor of the Welsh Baptist church at Edwardsville, Pennsylvania, visited Wales during the 1904–5 Revival and knew RB personally.[15] His church was in association with the Welsh Baptist Churches of North-eastern Pennsylvania. The secretary of this organisation was a son of Dr William Morris of Treorci, and it was from this group of churches that RB received a letter in 1906 inviting him to visit them. He left Porth in February 1907, taking with him a collection of hymns, *Prayer and Praise: Gweddi a Mawl*, a bilingual work that he had edited himself. During his absence his members prayed for him daily, and W. S. Jones kept an eye on them on his behalf.[16]

RB began his ministry in Edwardsville, a place that had experienced revival during the ministries of L. Ton Evans and J. T. Griffith. In the course of twelve months, J. T. Griffith had received a hundred people into membership.[17] RB's ministry at Edwardsville was severe, but many acknowledged that their lives would be different as a result of his visit. One member believed that the meetings were 'not as exciting as in Wales, but the change of life is just as intense and as real, I am sure'.[18]

The missioner also preached at Parsons, Pittston and Parish Street—three churches in Wilkesbarre, whose ministers were supportive.[19] He introduced the open-air service and the procession as means of witness—common occurrences in Wales but new to the Welsh churches in America. But it was his ministry at Scranton that was most powerful. During his stay there he preached on Romans 8:12, and his message on the theme of 'The Kingdom' was described as 'striking'.[20] He must have felt at home there: so many of his congregation were colliers from Wales, though at that time they were being forced to look for other work. A short while after he left them the chapel was set on fire, and there was a suspicion that this had something to do with RB's visit.[21]

During his time at Wilkesbarre he preached three other sermons based on Romans, chapter 8. His theme was 'The Works of the Spirit and the Works of the Flesh'.[22] Because of the flesh, churches had been brought down to the level of *eisteddfodau* and parties. Many had forfeited heaven by 'receiving the spirit in the power of the smoke and so slaying body and soul'.[23] This was a theme that he returned to continually during his ministry. He did not confine himself to Welsh churches, but visited English churches also, including some black congregations.

In America RB received criticism of the same nature as that levelled at him in Wales. Ironically, one of the chief critics was J. Cromwell Hughes, a Welshman and minister of Hyde Park, the church that in 1904 had invited RB to be their minister. The critic believed that 'the apostle of Keswick' demanded too much from congregations.[24] What was needed, rather, was more emphasis on grace and forgiveness. A few churches decided not to welcome his ministry a second time, and there were expressions of disapproval in both Providence and Wilkesbarre.

The church at Edwardsville, however, was full of praise for RB's ministry. The secretary of the church sent a long letter to him on his return to Wales.[25] It included a response to RB's refusal to return to Edwardsville as pastor, as well as praise for his ministry. The secretary informed him that they were still holding wonderful meetings. RB's preaching had affected many, especially the young people. In many of the meetings in Edwardsville, Pittston and Nanticoke, dozens of young people had testified of their spiritual experiences. The secretary had heard that even the young people of Hyde Park were determined to invite RB to return, 'regardless of difficulties'.[26]

Even as late as 1933, the year that RB died, tributes were paid to him because of his former ministry in America. Thanks were given to God for the visit. 'His clear, plain messages on Bible truth was a healing to our souls and will never be forgotten.'[27] Another person, equally complimentary, wrote:

> How I have praised God many times for sending him to America 25 years ago. That was when Calvary was made real to me and I shall not forget some of the messages, especially the one on the Potter and the Clay. That was the night I surrendered and became willing to be clay that God could [could] mold me. Everything changed after that.[28]

Churches had been blessed, and a lasting work of grace done in many hearts.

RB returned home to a rapturous welcome; according to Brynmor Jones, the welcome meeting was 'a big, emotional affair with W. S. Jones presiding'.[29] During his speech Dr William Morris, Treorci, expressed his opinion that the visit was 'the most effective mission ever conducted by a Welshman in America',[30] while L. Ton Evans ('Junius') was enraptured by the messages of 'this most Christlike of God's servants'.[31]

Home again

The minister of Ainon returned home not to rest but to work. He settled down quickly to the twin tasks of building his church and taking the gospel to other parts of the country.

He was still full of energy. Every aspect of the life of the church demanded attention.

One problem was the debt on the building; this amounted to between £600 and £700 and needed to be cleared. The church collected regularly, and eventually, in 1913–14, the sum was paid off. Sir William James Thomas, JP, proprietor of Ynys-hir Colliery, had promised to contribute to each church in Ynys-hir a sum equal to that collected by the church.[32] A week of prayer was arranged, and members were given slips of paper to record the value of the gift they intended to donate. The following Sunday the papers were collected, and the total sum announced was such that the congregation sang the Doxology.[33] Other promises were received, making the members even more optimistic. RB put up a chart in the vestry to plot the progress of the collection.[34] The members had promised £387, and other gifts brought the total to £546-13s-5d. Sir William James Thomas was happy not only to contribute what was needed to clear the debt but to double the total collected, as he had promised, so that the church was able to install central heating.

With the debt cleared, the church could now concentrate on helping others, especially in the work of supporting the ministry in weaker churches. RB not only told his people to give, but he also led by example. In the list of contributors towards the ministry in Ainon, only two or three members gave higher sums than the minister. There was need for careful stewardship by both church and pastor because, even when in 1909 the church was able to pay a fixed wage, this amounted to only £2 a week. Over a period of time this was raised to £3 and then to £5 a week.[35]

In March 1914 the church arranged Jubilee Meetings, when the guest speakers were Charles Davies (Cardiff),

W. S. Jones (Llwynypia) and Dr William Morris (Treorci).[36] In this year of Jubilee the church also marked an increase in membership. Considering the difficulties encountered, the membership had been quite steady. When RB commenced his ministry, it stood at about 80, but by 1913 the number had doubled to 167.[37] Many of the members were colliers, not earning high wages; but this was balanced by the fact that when war broke out in 1914, such men were not called up because of their occupation.

The pastor of Ainon was the last person to concentrate wholly on the local church. He had a passion for making the gospel known in as many areas as possible, at home and overseas. A later report in 1925 reminded his readers that 'His deepest desire was that the church might become a missionary one in the true and full sense of the word.'[38] Missionaries from different countries wrote to him, seeking advice, and in 1913 Ainon decided to adopt David Jones as their missionary. This was in response to a Baptist Missionary Society appeal entitled 'Station Plan'. David Jones was from Llwynhendy, Llanelli, and worked with the Baptist Missionary Society in Africa. He later left that Society to work with the Apostolic Church.[39] The church at Ainon set a target of £100 to be raised for Foreign Mission work during 1914, the Sunday school being responsible for collecting £30 to £40 of this total.[40]

31 August 1916

On 31 August 1916, RB was present at a valedictory service held at Ainon for a missionary leaving for Africa under the auspices of the Africa Inland Mission.[41] The service impressed both him and many of the young people of the church. Some of them consecrated themselves to the work of God, expressing willingness to go wherever he might lead. RB felt the need to equip them for this future work. What was the best way to do so? He believed that some provision could be supplied by the church itself.

Those who were engaged in Christian work, or were thinking of becoming so, were formed into a class, and RB met with them one evening a week.[42] These classes provided seasons of true worship. Several books were read together—books calculated to help those who wanted to enter Christian service.

After about two years of such meetings RB drew up a curriculum for the class. Almost immediately afterwards, Sidney Evans called to see RB. Evan Roberts's co-worker in the 1904–5 Revival had been called to a church in Porth, Rhondda, in 1916. He had been meeting with his young people in just the same way as RB had been doing at Ainon, but had found difficulty in drawing up a syllabus for them. RB showed him the one he had just prepared. It was 'the very thing' that Sidney Evans wanted. The two groups were formed into one class, meeting two nights a week, with each minister providing the teaching for one of the evenings.[43] A day or two after the decision was taken, a woman living not far from Ynys-hir wrote to RB expressing her desire to work overseas. A meeting was therefore arranged for all those interested in gospel work. Members of the two groups were present, together with RB's correspondent and five others who had responded to the invitation. Swift progress was being made.

> This took place about the end of 1918. The classes once started went on profitably, and still others from other parts joined as the weeks went by.[44]

Teachers and students became convinced that there was a need for more concentrated teaching. The answer, they believed, was to set up a day-school, but there were two great obstacles. The first, inevitably, was the need of financial help, and the second, the fact that Sidney Evans and his wife were convinced that they were called to work in India. RB, however, was certain that if the day-school was of God, Sidney Evans and his wife should not go to India. As it happened, the couple were delayed in their plans, so the two men were able to continue their work together. According to RB, the day-school was planned to commence in the autumn of 1919.[45]

Three considerations motivated RB to open this school. The first was the growing number of believers that wanted to enter full-time Christian service; the second, the encouragement he received from the increase at that time in the number of Faith Missionary Societies formed; and the third, the shift in the denominational colleges towards theological modernism. RB did not name any particular college but believed that the trend was evident. In 1896, T. Witton Davies had been appointed lecturer at the Bangor Baptist College; he was later to be a contributor to A. S. Peake's *Commentary of the Bible*. In 1897, E. O. Davies, an influential liberal, had been appointed lecturer at the Calvinistic Methodist College at Bala, and in the same year Thomas Lewis was appointed lecturer at Brecon Congregational College, becoming Principal in 1907. Lewis did much to spread the higher critical view of the Old Testament. In 1908, J. Morgan Jones began his work as lecturer at the Bangor Congregational College and was made Principal in 1926. He was deeply influenced by the teaching of Harnack.[46]

In 1919, as RB faced this new task of establishing a Bible school, he received, and accepted, a call to the pastorate of Tabernacle English Baptist Church, Porth. Before continuing with the story of the day-school and of his move to Porth, we need to consider other aspects of his ministry during the period from 1904 to 1919.

5
Confirming and developing

During the period from 1907 to 1919, RB laboured continuously in organising Christian conventions and finding new means of teaching and evangelising. Over these years he kept in close contact with the Keswick Conference leaders.

Conventions

Many of the Keswick leaders were to reunite at the annual convention in Cardiff in 1907. Evan Hopkins, F. B. Meyer, E. L. Hamilton and Jessie Penn-Lewis were among the speakers at those meetings.[1] Another very significant convention was held at Leicester in 1908. RB, Evan Roberts and Jessie Penn-Lewis took part, and the theme was 'Revival'. 'The Thursday afternoon meeting especially was in glorious revival power and liberty.'[2] RB, Jessie Penn-Lewis and George Litchfield (of the Keswick Deputation to Japan) were to have appointed the chairpersons for the Convention, but they decided to leave the chair empty in order to signify that the Holy Spirit was in charge. F. B. Meyer joined them for some of the meetings. Evan Roberts was present at all the sessions, 'and on the last day he was manifestly led of God in taking the lead in all the meetings'.[3]

After the convention Jessie Penn-Lewis received a letter from F. Kehl, India.[4] A Mrs Kalvington from England had sent him a letter criticising aspects of the Leicester Convention, based on a report in *The Life of Faith*. The criticisms are not expressed clearly, but the suggestion is that she was unhappy with 'the Holy Ghost chair movement' and had queried the 'manifestations' in the meetings. She had also written to Evan Roberts:

> Mr Roberts knows all—for she wrote to him—but he is working by prayer and I believe that his prayers have guarded you from making a terrible mistake by passing on Mrs Kalvington's letter to anyone else.[5]

F. Kehl was one of many links that Jessie Penn-Lewis had in India. She exerted considerable influence on evangelicals in that land.[6]

A month later RB was at another convention, again in the company of Jessie Penn-Lewis and F. B. Meyer. They were the speakers at the first Swansea Convention, held in St Andrews Church, St. Helen's Road.[7] A Thursday 'Over-Tea Meeting' was arranged, costing 4d per person. Time was given to prayer and praise, and Jessie Penn-Lewis spoke on *The Word of the Cross* booklet. RB must have been pleased that the hymn-book chosen for use was his own collection of hymns, *Prayer and Praise/Gweddi a Mawl* (1907). He himself spoke on three aspects of sanctification: 'Are we temples or prisons of the Holy Spirit?', 'The hopelessness of living in the flesh', and 'The Secret of True Liberty—Alive unto God'. There were large gatherings at these meetings, especially on the last evening.[8]

The Llandrindod Convention was still popular. RB was appointed to the Council of Reference in 1907 and spoke three times in the 1908 meetings. Once again he majored on consecration and separation. He challenged the congregations to yield themselves to God—not only their hearts but their bodies also.

> As those challenging words rang out, observers saw many men throwing away their pipes and women

casting down their vanity cases. One was heard praying, 'Lord, now I have given the last key in the bunch.'[9]

RB must have been delighted, in that praise was leading onwards to obedience.

At the 1911 Llandrindod Convention, RB's theme was 'The Kingdom'. The way to live in the kingdom was to behold the King. He was taken up with presenting the Lord Jesus Christ:

> Behold the Lord! This means spiritual intercourse between God and Man, a constant commerce between the heart and Jesus. It means appreciating Him, choosing Him, yielding to Him, trusting Him, and appropriating Him by faith. All this, and more, is beholding Him. Our eyes must constantly be on Him and not on His work within us, for introspection is fatal to spiritual growth.[10]

This was a fine Christ-centred message.

Many conventions were inaugurated during the period immediately after 1907—those at Rhymney, Aberdare, Pontypridd, Pontymoile and Bridgend, for example. Some of these were conducted through the medium of Welsh, others in English, and some bilingual.

One of the main centres in south Wales was Llanelli, and RB was among the speakers at the first convention held there in 1913.[11] The local arrangements were made by Trevor Jones, Bethania, whom RB knew from his years of ministering in the town. Most of the prominent revival leaders took part in these meetings—W. W. Lewis, Nantlais Williams, W. S. Jones, David Evans, and singers Sam Jenkins, Griffith Hughes and T. Conwil Evans. Altogether about twenty persons took part. The convention was delighted with Griffith Hughes's rendering of a few psalms with organ accompaniment.[12] This 1913 series of meetings established support for a convention in Llanelli, a predominantly Welsh town, for many years to come.

The Ammanford Convention

When a convention was organised for Ammanford in 1917, it very soon developed as the preferred annual gathering for many children of the revival and others. It was the brain-child of Nantlais Williams. J. D. Williams suggests three reasons why Nantlais was moved to inaugurate the convention.[13] Firstly, he was still under the influence of the 1904–5 Revival. New and older converts needed teaching, and there was need also to keep them united. Secondly, Nantlais had been deeply influenced by the Keswick-in-Wales Conference, as also by the Keswick meetings themselves, which he had attended in 1909 and 1914. And lastly, 1917 was the bicentenary of the birth of the hymn-writer William Williams, Pantycelyn. Nantlais was enthralled by the depth of his spiritual experience and believed that conventions could be the means of deepening the spiritual lives of believers in the twentieth century.[14]

Nantlais wrote to RB early in 1917, expressing his desire for a convention. RB replied by return of post, noting his agreement and adding that if Nantlais would not organise one, he would do so himself. Nantlais proceeded with the arrangements, despite the fact that the Free Church Council was not too happy with such a venture in wartime. Many were sceptical. Some believed that the minister of Bethany was in league with the Church of England; others that he was in league with the Plymouth Brethren—and Nantlais himself would not have been surprised had a few believed he was in league with the Devil![15]

Meetings were arranged for the period 15-18 May 1917. RB was preaching the previous Sunday at Ebeneser

Welsh Baptist church, Ammanford, and staying at a house next door to Nantlais's home.[16] So they were able to discuss the meetings of the coming week, at which RB was one of the speakers. Most of the sessions were held at Bethany Chapel, and were in Welsh. The usual Welsh convention speakers took part: RB, W. S. Jones, W. W. Lewis, Keri Evans and O. M. Owen (who had by now moved to Birkenhead). Talbot Rice, a Swansea vicar and a popular speaker at Llandrindod, preached at the English service in All Saints' Church. On the last night, All Saints', Ebeneser and Bethany were full of expectant worshippers. Nantlais rejoiced that Nonconformist ministers, Anglican clergy and Apostolic Church leaders were to be found together in harmony.[17]

RB was back in Ammanford the following year, when another of the speakers was J. H. Williams, Porthmadog, a prominent leader in Anglesey during the 1904–5 Revival. North and south were linked together once again. In 1919 he was again asked to speak, and he delivered addresses on *Yr Ail-ddyfodiad yn ei berthynas â Theyrnas Duw a'r Cenhedloedd, a'r Iddewon a'r Eglwys* (The Second Coming in its relation to the Kingdom of God and the Gentiles, and the Jews and the Church).[18] He later published these messages as a book, under the title *Yr Ail-ddyfodiad yng ngoleuni'r Epistolau at y Thesaloniaid* (The Second Coming in the light of the Epistles to the Thessalonians). Again, most of these meetings were conducted in Welsh.

The first speaker to be invited to Ammanford from outside Wales arrived in 1920.[19] He was George Grubb, London, and very soon others followed. This meant that more meetings were held in English, but for a number of years the Welsh meetings remained in the majority. Another regular feature that first appeared during the early years was the missionary meeting. The 1920 missionary meeting was led by Huxley Thomas, Ammanford, home on furlough from north-east India. The missionary meeting of the 1921 Convention was outstanding.[20] As a result of an appeal made by Rees Howells on behalf of the Portugese East Africa Mission, a lady got up and promised a gift of £1,200. This was for the purchase of a farm, so as to establish a foothold in that country. At the same meeting a husband and wife volunteered to oversee the farm.[21]

These missionary meetings were significant for other reasons: they provided information on missionaries in different parts of the world; missionaries from far-flung countries attended them, and all present were challenged as to their own responsibility towards overseas mission work. The Ammanford Convention, other local conventions and the Llandrindod meetings contributed substantially to the support of mission work both at home and abroad. RB gave wholehearted support to every type of venture aimed at spreading the gospel.

Yr Efengylydd

In this period of his life RB was often the main speaker at conventions and preaching festivals, and his experience in 1908 in this regard was no exception. He preached at his mother church, Hebron (Dowlais),[22] at Treherbert, at Pen-clawdd with Keri Evans, at Bryn-mawr in the south and Holyhead in the north.[23] He also spoke at the Llandrindod Convention.

But in that same year other means of teaching and witnessing opened up to him. A new magazine was presented to the people of Wales. The idea of a magazine originated with Cynog Williams (Trecynon, Aberdare), when in 1908 he, together with Trevor Jones (Llanelli) and Joseph James (Cwm-bach, Aberdare), produced *The Mill Street*

Magazine. It was renamed *Yr Efengylydd* (The Evangelist). Containing an inset, *The Home Messenger*, the whole magazine comprised only a few pages.[24]

A group of ministers met in Noddfa, Treorci, to discuss the future development of this magazine. RB was appointed editor, O. M. Owen treasurer, and R. S. Morris (Cwmafan) to receive orders and payments. It was decided not to include advertisements, and this decision was confirmed when a well-wisher sent a gift to cover all costs. An appeal was also made for funds in order to distribute free copies.[25]

A survey of *Yr Efengylydd* for 1909 reveals its nature and purpose: it aimed to deepen the spiritual lives of believers. Most of the Revival stalwarts are found among the contributors: RB, Charles Davies (Cardiff), E. Keri Evans (Carmarthen), W. S. Jones (Llwynypia), O. M. Owen (Liverpool), Nantlais Williams, Seth Joshua and Evan Roberts. The majority of the articles were in Welsh, with seven English contributions, one of these, *Ministry-obstructing Fever* (July 1909), written by Seth Joshua.

RB's editorials reveal his favourite themes—*Fullness of the Spirit* (April), *Revival* (August) and *Evangelism* (September). The November issue included a response to the Berlin Declaration that had condemned the emerging Pentecostal Movement. RB could not agree with everything in the Declaration but emphasised that it was a warning to all Christians to be watchful and prayerful. During 1909, RB received contributions from over thirty authors, including one woman, Mrs Beresford Baker. She was the wife of Captain William Beresford Baker, a well-known sportsman in Dover, Kent. He had bought a number of properties, and the income from these enabled his wife to open a rest-home and a book-room. She was related to the Derry-Ormond family of Cardiganshire.[26] RB and other

Christian leaders spent some time in her home, especially during periods of physical tiredness. D. S. Jones stayed with her during a period of stress, and wrote to RB,

> This lady is a dear child of God, who seems to be bent on living a purely spiritual life, lifting the poor &c. But she has to bear the penalty of ostracisation, bitter hatred, misunderstandings, backbiting, calumny, on part of the dead churches around her.[27]

During the following years the number of female contributors slowly increased.

In keeping with the aim of the magazine, a number of articles dealt with the theme of sanctification. The most important contribution was received from J. H. Williams, who wrote four articles on *Yr Efengyl yn galw am Sancteiddrwydd* (The Gospel calling for Sanctification). The first of these appeared in January 1909. W. S. Jones complemented this series with an article dealing with the practical aspects of sanctification (January), as did Evan Roberts's article, *Y Groes Feunyddiol* (The Daily Cross). E. Keri Evans adopted a different method, basing his five articles, *Bywyd ac Athroniaeth* (Life and Philosophy), on philosophical points. In his first contribution (January 1909) he approached the question 'What must I do to be saved?' in three ways. A metaphysician would ask the question, 'What is the nature of being saved?' A psychologist might ask, 'What happens when I am saved?' But the response of the Christian is that of faith. It is only a response of faith that will result in the experience of salvation. This does not mean that the mind is neglected. Although it is but a servant to faith, yet it is useful and necessary and, when used correctly, can aid faith to face the challenge of the metaphysician and the psychologist.

Keri Evans developed his argument in the remaining four articles (January, March, June and December). To have included more articles of this nature would have been unwise, for Keri Evans had an exceptionally sharp mind; but it would have strengthened the witness of *Yr Efengylydd* had it dealt more often and in more detail with doctrinal problems. There were exceptions later—the contributions of John Thomas especially, dealing with theological and critical developments. The main doctrinal contributions were provided by D. Wynne Evans, one of the men who paved the way for Llandrindod, 1903. He devoted nine articles to *Ail-ddyfodiad ein Harglwydd Iesu* (The Second Coming of our Lord Jesus), presented from a premillennial point of view (January to November, 1909). This teaching was to be a continuing feature of the magazine.

The theme of revival was not neglected, and David Hughes, Pontycymer, reminded readers of the 1904–5 Revival in a series of six articles (January to November), *Bendithion Arosol y Diwygiad* (The Abiding Blessings of the Revival). Three biographical sketches were included in 1909—on Adoniram Judson (February), Dr Baedeker (February), and Howell Harris (June). There were a few articles on Welsh history in the coming years, but not as many as might be expected in a magazine produced in Wales and springing from the 1904–5 Revival. Trevor Jones, Llanelli, made a valuable contribution (January to September); he dealt with biblical themes in *Trem ar Lyfrau'r Beibl* (A Survey of the Books of the Bible). Also included, at times, were a few hymns and some poetry.

RB was editor until 1916, when Nantlais Williams joined him as co-editor. There was no marked change in content during the whole of the period from 1909 to 1919. The number of missionary articles increased, and many missionaries sent in reports. The editor was glad to hear from David Jones (Africa), Rees Howells (Africa), Henry Rees (India), Daniel Thomas (South America) and Watkin Roberts of the Thado-Kookie Mission, India.[28] These men all worked with Faith Missions.

RB's personal discipline, and the faithful help of others, ensured the success of *Yr Efengylydd*. It was a much-needed provision for Welsh-reading believers of the period.

A new venture

While preaching in Dolgellau, north Wales, during March 1909, R. B. Jones received a letter from someone offering a Gospel Van for evangelistic work in Wales. She wrote as a 'daughter of the King'.[29] The evangelist was very much aware of the possibilities of such work. Explaining the background to the readers of the *Efengylydd,* he reminded them of the increase in different sports, the lack of young people in the churches, and the presence of too many public houses in the country. The influence of doctrinal heresy was also being felt in the churches. If Robert Blatchford's socialist paper the *Clarion* had its van, then surely the *Efengylydd* had more reason for such a vehicle in service of the gospel. Favourable responses to the offer were received from Nantlais Williams and Keri Evans.[30]

Further information was given in *Yr Efengylydd*. The 'child of the King' was Mrs Agnes Hollins, Cardiff.[31] She explained how she had visited the home of Evan Roberts in Loughor, and Evan's brother Dan had expressed the need for evangelism in Wales. She, in turn, mentioned this need to a friend of hers who had seen an advertisement in *The Christian* offering a Gospel Van for a reasonable price. This was the story behind her letter to RB in Dolgellau.

O. M. Owen, who was preaching with RB in the Dolgellau meetings, volunteered to travel to Warrington to inspect the vehicle. His report was favourable and the van started its journey to Wales, arriving at Llandrindod the week of the annual convention. The connection with the magazine was evident from the name it was given— *Cerbyd Yr Efengylydd* (The Evangelist's Chariot).

Many ministers promised their active support. In its first months of itinerating the following served with the van:[32]

M. P. Evans, Abertridwr	16-20 Aug.
T. D. Morris, Warrior Run, and	
Mr E. Richards, Ton	23-27 Aug.
R. B. Jones, Porth	30 Aug.-3 Sept.
J. R. Evans, Llwynhendy	6-10 Sept.
W. W. Lewis, Swansea	13-17 Sept
W. S. Jones, Llwynypia	20-24 Sept.
W. Nantlais Williams, Ammanford	27 Sept.–1 Oct.
Trefor Jones, Llanelli	4-8 Oct.
E. Keri Evans, Carmarthen, and	
Sam Jenkins, Llanelli	11-15 Oct.
R. S. Morris, Cwmafan	16-29 Oct.
W. G. Hill, Maesteg	1-5 Nov.

All on this list had been zealous workers during the 1904–5 Revival, and most of them were by now prominent leaders. Over half of them were Baptists. By this time a strong Baptist group had emerged around the leadership of RB and W. S. Jones.

William T. Evans from Pontypridd committed himself to the full-time work of missioner and was set apart for the work on 5 August 1909.[33] A prayer meeting in the afternoon was followed by an evening service in which W. S. Jones gave the address. Charles Davies (Cardiff) and Seth Joshua also took part. Before the end of the month, RB had joined the Gospel Van, and was ministering with William Evans and T. D. Morris (Warrior Run, America) at Llangadog and Llandeilo, Carmarthenshire. During this tour, the evangelists were accompanied by Mrs Hollins of Cardiff.[34] They depended on friendly farmers to supply horses to take the van from one place to another. During 1910, the van was in the Rhondda for a period, and this provided RB with another opportunity to help. J. T. Phillips, (Bethany, Ynys-hir), who had assisted RB at Ainon, also joined the team.[35]

It is surprising how much of Wales was covered during these early years of evangelism. Periods were spent at Harlech and Caernarfon, Llanfyllin and Llandrindod, Pembroke and the Rhondda. Such travelling called for patient endurance. William T. Evans found the work too demanding, and Robert Roberts and Griffith Hughes took his place.[36]

The two new workers were anxious to work with the Gospel Van throughout the year, but this proved impossible. Because of Robert Roberts's ill health, Griffith Hughes had to work alone during 1913, but a number of ministers joined him in the ministry for different periods. Regular appeals were made over the years in *Yr Efengylydd* for the financial support of Griffith Hughes and his family.[37]

A tour of Cardiganshire during 1913 illustrates the nature of the work and the help received by ministers (RB included). Aberystwyth was made the main centre for the first part of the tour, with visits to Llanbadarn and Penparcau. At Llanbadarn, a large number of children gathered round the missioner, followed by many adults. The children were then led in procession through the streets.[38] During the three weeks' stay at Aberystwyth, David Evans and D. S. Jones, both from Bridgend, helped Griffith Hughes. During their last meeting in the town

many were humbled by the Spirit of God and sponta-
neously fell on their knees in prayer and praise.

A three-hour journey took the missioner to *Cwrdd
Gweddi'r Mynydd* (The Mountain Prayer Meeting),
formed as a result of the 1904–5 Revival. Three meetings
were held during the day, during which about 1,500 people
attended. Considering the lonely, rural nature of the location (near Llangwyryfon, Cardiganshire), this number was
amazingly high. During the evening meeting many were
on their knees praying, some crying and others praising.
The meeting lasted for three hours.[39]

A kind friend provided four horses to move the van to
its next destination. When they arrived at Llanrhystud,
the owner of the Black Lion invited them to stand outside
the hotel. At Llanrhystud, Llan-non and Aber-arth the
children were again led in procession through the streets.
RB and Trevor Jones (Llanelli) preached during the visit
to Llan-non.[40]

Griffith Hughes had a break in early August, during
which he attended the Llandrindod Convention, but immediately after the convention he was on the move again. He
returned to Aber-arth, where Keri Evans joined him.
Aberaeron was crowded during the holiday period and
there, on Sunday 17 August, a crowd of about 1,500 listened to Griffith Hughes, W. W. Lewis and David Evans.[41]
The evangelists were greatly encouraged—encouragement
that was much needed, for they were receiving considerable criticism for their methods of evangelism. Further
encouragements were received at Llanarth, where Griffith
Hughes received gifts of potatoes, meat, eggs and butter.
At New Quay the home missioners were inspired by the
knowledge that they were labouring in the town where
Joseph Jenkins had ministered. They knew that his God
was still at work.[42]

A portable hall

After Robert Roberts had recovered from ill health, the two home missioners became more conscious of the need to develop their methods for taking the gospel to the people of Wales. This need was made known in the pages of *Yr Efengylydd*, together with the information that the cost of a portable wooden hall would be about £80.[43] Only five responses were received during October–November 1912, and these included a gift of £1 from 'RBJ' (Rhys Bevan Jones).[44] By the end of the next month, however, the number of contributions had increased, amounting to £27-11-7. One lady sent ten shillings (50p) of her pension money, whilst a young lad in a workhouse somehow managed to send a gift. As another contributor was on his way to post a gift of half a crown (12½p), he met a friend who, when informed of the need, provided a further ten shillings.[45]

A portable wooden hall was purchased and was first erected at Pontarddulais on 11 December 1913. As well as using the hall, the missioners arranged meetings, whenever possible, in various chapels. Usually these were well attended. This was true of the meetings held at Llangennech, Carmarthenshire, when RB and J.T. Phillips (Ynys-hir) were the preachers.[46] Griffith Hughes also believed in the value of visiting the homes of an area. The same pattern was followed during tours in the county from 1914 to 1916, when the missioners visited Llandovery, Carmarthen town and the Gwendraeth Valley. Nor was north Wales neglected.[47] Griffith Hughes spent some weeks in Holyhead during 1915, where David Lloyd (Hebron) was happy to receive him.

During the war years (1914–18) there was also opportunity to minister to soldiers. The Hall was set up for a period near the Newton Barracks in Porthcawl. At this time, too, RB found another helper for Griffith Hughes,[48] in the person of D. J. Davies, originally from Dowlais, who had returned from America. Soldiers came to the Hall, and the missioners visited The Rest, a home where wounded soldiers back from France and the Dardanelles were convalescing. The matron and nurses also attended meetings.[49] Griffith Hughes persevered in these labours with van and hall until his retirement in 1919.

The year 1919 became a very significant one for RB. The decision had been taken to establish the day-school, and this work had to be undertaken whilst commencing a new ministry at Tabernacle, Porth. The day-school opened in September 1919, and RB replied accepting the call to Tabernacle on the 28th of the same month.[50] The local paper heralded his coming with glowing tributes. A 'powerful preacher' was coming to Tabernacle, having 'an attractive personality in the pulpit'.[51] His reputation would soon surpass that of all the chapel's previous ministers.

The reporter believed that the new minister savoured too much of 'other worldliness' and 'monkish detachment', and yet was quick to add that 'Mr Jones's austere purity is communicable'.[52] Sporting activities and Sabbath-breaking were on the increase, and there was need to stem the tide. RB was exactly the person to call people to repentance and holy living.

6
Tabernacle, Porth

On moving to Tabernacle, Hannah Street, Porth, RB must have felt at home immediately, for Salem Chapel, where he had previously ministered (from 1899 to 1904), stood at the bottom of the same street. During the years of his ministries at Salem and Ainon there had been many changes. Houses had been built on Hannah Street's open spaces, and a cinema had been erected—a matter of grave concern to Tabernacle's minister. During this period, too, great numbers of people had moved into the Rhondda Valley seeking work. Behind Tabernacle, a stream named 'The Feeder' ran towards the railway and the Hafod coal-pits, providing the hydraulic power that worked the pits.[1] Tabernacle, just like Hebron—RB's home church at Dowlais—was by now surrounded by signs of change and development.

During the early years of the influx, the majority of newcomers arriving at Porth and the Rhondda were Welsh-speaking; but slowly the situation changed. By 1911, while the majority of the Valley population spoke both English and Welsh, 60,056 out of a population of 152,781 spoke only English. The non-Welsh-speakers, like the Welsh-speakers before them, were conscious of the need to worship in their own language, and between 1867 and 1892 five English-speaking causes sprang up in Porth. Both the Wesleyan and the Primitive Methodist churches were formed in 1867.[2] Some of the Welsh churches resented the intrusion of English causes. When, for instance, John Pugh

of the Forward Movement tried to introduce English services at the Calvinistic Methodist church in Porth during the
1880s, one Welsh-speaking cause strongly opposed him.[3]
Success was not achieved until 1892. An English-speaking
Congregationalist work was established in 1881.

Tabernacle and the call to R. B. Jones

In 1872 there were only a handful of English Baptists in
Porth. For a brief period they worshipped with the
Wesleyans, but they also met separately for fellowship in a
room not far from Dinas Station. Opportunity then arose
for them to meet in various cottages before eventually
finding a home in the Llanwonno Board Schoolroom.
Unlike John Pugh's experiences, these English-speaking
Baptists had the support of their Welsh-speaking denominational brethren. The cause was established in 1874, a
building was obtained in 1875, and Tabernacle Chapel was
opened in 1877.[4]

David Thomas, the first minister, worked as a part-time
weaver to supplement his salary.[5] The second minister,
John Davies, died after only a few months in the post.[6]
Owen Owens, who followed as the third minister, emphasised the place of prayer and Bible study in the life of the
church. Two branch churches, Bethany, Ynys-hir, and
Penuel, Trehafod, were established.[7] During the ministry of
W. E. Prince, the fourth pastor at Tabernacle, the practice
of holding prayer meetings in different homes was begun;
the church received many new additions (a result of
1904–5 Revival), and the church building was extended. It
was with heavy hearts that the church parted with their
minister in 1908.[8] Their first recourse was to R. B. Jones,
then ministering at Ainon, Ynys-hir; he was invited to be
W. E. Prince's successor, but at that time he had been only
five years at Ainon and declined the invitation.[9]

T. W. Hart accepted a call to be the fifth minister of Tabernacle and stayed for three years. There were ominous signs of decline when he arrived, but he was the means not only of stopping the decline but of renewing the spiritual life of the church.[10] Another four years passed before the next minister was called. Having invited RB in 1909 and considered him again shortly afterwards (without however proceeding to a call), the church eventually proffered a unanimous call to him in 1919.[11] RB accepted and agreed to commence his ministry on Sunday 23 November 1919. The induction services took place on that Sunday and a number of other meetings were held the following week. W. S. Jones (Llwynypia), Dr William Morris (Treorci), and Charles Davies (Cardiff) took part in the induction.[12]

The nature of his ministry
On the first Sunday in December, RB had opportunity to preach on one of his favourite themes, the Second Coming of the Lord Jesus Christ. An individual from Porth had predicted the end of the world in December 1919. In his sermon, the new minister declared that an end of the world would never occur, but rather 'the consummation of the age'. The coming of Christ would realise the millennium age leading to a new heaven and a new earth.[13]

When RB moved to Porth, he faced two huge tasks. He had to lead the work in the church at Tabernacle, and he had to develop the Bible School newly opened in September 1919. We will consider the progress of the church before giving attention to the latter.

The church bought 'Gwernlwyn', the Ainon Manse, as a home for RB and his family. He pointed out that there was need for an assistant in the church and he was given authority to make an appointment. RB's choice was Sister Sutherland of the Faith Mission of Scotland, and she commenced her work in September 1920. The new minister buckled down to the task of pastoring a church of 260 members.[14]

He was determined to develop every aspect of the life of the church, including its finance. Owing to the increasing attendance there was immediate need to enlarge the building.[15] Promises of donations were invited from the members, and on Sunday evening 5 December 1920 a memorable communion service was held, when members brought forward their promise forms, whilst Watts's hymn, 'When I survey the wondrous cross', was being sung. The astonishing sum of £4,300 was promised there and then, and by 1924 the total was to reach £5,000. Such a response must have pleased RB greatly; one of his greatest fears always was lack of commitment.

Services and discipline

The members of Tabernacle responded not only financially but also in terms of faithfulness to the services. On Sundays a prayer meeting was held at 9.45 a.m., followed by the morning service at 10.45. There was an afternoon Sunday school, which by 1924 had 829 names on its register. Nearly 1,000 people attended the evening service, enthralled by RB's powerful, passionate preaching.[16] During the week, a prayer meeting, Bible study, children's meetings, Women's League, and Young People's Guild were held. Prayer was essential for every department of the work.[17]

The prayer meeting was given a unique status. It was organically linked to all aspects of church life—planning of work, business negotiations, visitation work and all emergencies. There were many other gatherings during the week: a network of cottage meetings, workmen's meetings, officers' meeting, and even a pastoral meeting. Nor were the activities of these meetings merely routine, for their participants were a mixture of godly veterans of the Revival, very sincere young people, and zealous students.

Prayers could be fervent and bold. One student acknowledged that to be in such a prayer meeting was something entirely new to her:

> At first I was a little shocked that people could speak in such a familiar way to God.[18]

In the Sunday morning service, when the children were present, and in some week-night meetings, use was made of visual aids such as Lantern Lectures. The most significant examples were RB's 'Demonstrations'. As a result of the training he had received at the works in Dowlais and with the Fawcett Company in Penydarren, RB had become a very competent model-maker. With the help of a few others, he constructed models to illustrate themes from the Bible. Topics included *The Church*, *The Story of the Ten Plagues*, *The Bible*, *Jubilee* and (most elaborate of all) *The Tabernacle in the Wilderness*. With the help of William Redwood, a local carpenter, RB made 'a scale model of the pavilion complete with altars, candlesticks, curtains and the Ark of the Covenant'.[19]

This *Demonstration of the Tabernacle*, with its forty different parts, was a considerable presentation.[20] It took the form of a service, and the aspect of worship was emphasised particularly in the opening sections. A reciter would introduce the theme. A soloist would sing, followed by a quartet. The story of the journey from Egypt to Sinai would then be summarised and a plan of the Tabernacle revealed. Every detail of its construction would be referred to, even the four different types of covering. As far as the 'ram's skin dyed red' was concerned, RB had no doubt as to its significance: 'Once again we meet with Christ'.[21]

RB spiritualised many aspects of the story, but the *Demonstration* was a means of teaching and worshipping. The dramatic aspects could be very effective. This was especially true of *The Tabernacle in the Wilderness*. With the cry, 'It is finished',

> a hidden helper drew apart the curtains and switched on a powerful diffused light symbolizing the Shekinah around and over the Ark.[22]

There are a few people at Tabernacle presently who still remember the demonstrations of the latter period of RB's ministry.

The pastor, regarded by some as stern and serious, was a very effective teacher of children. He and the church took care of them from the cradle, making detailed arrangements for their needs. Parents would dedicate their children to God and vow to raise them according to Christian principles. Brynmor Pierce Jones describes the development from dedication to later years:

> Placed on the Cradle Roll, that child would be brought regularly until old enough to join in choruses and lisp words after the leader. Soon the child will bring its own Bible and be able to recite 'God is Love' or 'I am the Good Shepherd'. Then he would begin to learn the catechism, understand the talks, repeat Golden Texts and walk out to ring the Birthday Bell or receive a medal for good attendance. At nine years old he has won prize books, mastered the 'Sword Drill', and amassed a store of tales from the gifted teachers.[23]

The main emphasis was on teaching, and children would be grouped according to age. On occasion, opportunities were given for them to respond personally. Both the church and RB believed that children could come to faith in Christ.

The quotation above mentions the catechism. This was composed by RB and entitled *The Children's Bible School.* It was one of the main methods at Tabernacle for instructing the children and had a simple format of brief questions and answers.[24] It summarised the truths of the Christian faith and trained the memory. Its four parts were: Baptism, Bible, Old Testament and New Testament. Each section was divided into chapters, and a single chapter might contain as many as sixty questions and answers.

The section on baptism included the main doctrines of the faith and of the way of salvation. A large part of this section concentrated on the nature of baptism. RB was quite clear regarding its nature and mode. The baptised should make a confession of repentance and faith in Christ. One question refers to 'sprinkling', and the answer is adamant that such a baptism is impossible. The next question 'Why is baptism by sprinkling impossible?' has the answer, 'Baptism and sprinkling are two entirely different things.' RB evidently felt the need to be even clearer:

Question: Is sprinkling a sin?
Answer: Sprinkling is a sin because it sets aside the ordinances of Christ.[25]

There was no option as to the mode of baptism; it had to be immersion.

Question: Is there baptism without immersion?
Answer: Without immersion there is no baptism.

Tabernacle Chapel was very ready to dedicate babies to God, and RB believed that all who died in infancy went to heaven because Christ had died for them. From an early age, therefore, the children would be grounded in one doctrine of baptism. All other traditions were ignored.

Aware that the Old Testament could be difficult for the children, RB sought to make the questions and answers in this section as helpful as possible. He divided the book into History, Poetry and Prophecy, and the questions show his interest in the formation of the Bible as well as in its content. He accepted its history as history, its poetry as poetry, and its prophecy as prophecy.[26]

R. B. Jones gave attention to the children of his church from the very beginning of his ministry. A secretary of Tabernacle bears witness to his contribution in this field:

> One of the first things he did, was to organize a 'Sunday Service and Bible League' for boys and girls. The membership soon reached 400, with average attendance at the morning service of 300, each member carrying a Bible and a hymnbook. Half an hour of the service was for them. He sought to ground them in the facts of Scripture, and make clear to them the way of salvation.[27]

A large company of young people met weekly at the church. These youngsters, together with the children, were provided with good literature. A children's library with a large turnover of books was established. Both young people and children studied Bunyan's *Pilgrim's Progress*,[28] and a number of periodicals were received by the congregation. The most popular bore the title *The King's Business*. Although RB was responsible for the content of the teaching of the various children's and young people's meetings, he had the able support of faithful teachers. He would encourage members to use their gifts in the different departments of the church.

RB, with the elders, deacons and Miss Sutherland (followed by a Miss Ellis) supervised the whole life of the church. Tabernacle had a church covenant and RB made sure that it was kept. It called for regular attendance, faithful giving, and submission to the decisions of the church. The leaders and the candidates for the ministry at home or overseas were tested doctrinally, whilst candidates for baptism were required to make a confession of personal faith in Jesus Christ. The deacons and Miss Sutherland, helped by district visitors, reported back to RB regarding the personal behaviour of members. Those going to the cinema or to sports meetings or attending any secular event would be reminded of the pledge they took on becoming members. When necessary, discipline would be administered.

The church workers also ministered to the sick and sorrowing. During a time of industrial unrest, as in 1926, more money would be laid aside for the Poor Fund, and representatives of the Women's Meeting would visit homes with gifts of fruit and eggs.[29]

The Annual Church Meeting was an important opportunity for surveying the work of the church. It was a serious but joyous occasion. A preaching service would be held in the afternoon, followed by a cup of tea. At 5.30 p.m. the church would meet for prayer, in preparation for the Church Meeting proper. Nine detailed reports were then usually given. A word of encouragement would be preached from the Scriptures, and finally members would gather around the Lord's Table, to be reminded again that the cross was at the centre of their faith.[30]

The Monthly Lecture and Weekly Bible School
Apart from regular church meetings, RB arranged a weekly Bible School and a monthly Lecture. Many from surrounding areas attended these meetings. The lectures

involved considerable preparation, as is evident from the variety of subjects discussed. Early examples were 'Our Lord and His Bible', 'Francis of Assisi', 'The Protestant Reformation' and 'The Clapham Sect'.[31] RB would then use the lectures again in the Bible Training School.

Topics for the weekly Bible School were also varied, but here more time would be spent studying books of the Bible. RB would deal with sections of the Bible at a time. One session of the School, for example, was devoted to the Pentateuch.[32] When dealing with Leviticus, he explained its significance. It was a manual for priest and people and had its fulfilment in the New Testament, as explained in the Letter to the Hebrews. He then gave an overview of the Book:

1. The Ground of Fellowship, chapters 1-7
2. The Medium of Fellowship, chapters 8-10
3. The Dangers of Fellowship, chapters 11-14
4. The Obstacles of Fellowship, chapter 16
5. Moral Accompaniments of Fellowship, chapters 17-22
6. The Fruit of Fellowship, chapter 23
7. The Obedience of Fellowship, chapters 24-27.[33]

RB's method, when teaching from the Letter to the Romans, was to consider a verse as found in the Revised Version and then compare it with that in the Authorised Version. He would discuss key words in the original Greek and bring out the meaning of the text and its context. Other subjects dealt with in the Bible School were 'Roman Catholicism', 'The Coming of Christ: When will it be?' and 'Mahomet'.[34] His book, *Spiritism in Bible Light*, was also the fruit of these lectures. The weekly Bible School and monthly Lecture confirmed the teaching of the regular meetings of the church and extended RB's influence in south

Wales and further afield. An associated correspondence course helped those who could not attend the School and extended its influence further.

Mission work

The work of the gospel was not confined to Tabernacle. RB's missionary zeal was still burning brightly and he continued to travel to conventions and evangelistic services. He spoke at conventions in Cardiff in 1921 and 1924 and continued to attend Llandrindod, where he was the main speaker in 1925.

In that same year, he gave the main addresses at the Ammanford Whitsun convention on 'His Lord's Money' and published them later in the year.[35] In 1926 he spoke again at Llandrindod. His theme on that occasion was 'The blood in the Book of Revelation', and it was developed in four addresses: (1) Revelation 1:5, 'Wash and loosen'; (2) Revelation 5:9, 'The service of Jesus's people'; (3) Revelation 7:14, 'Holy character'; (4) Revelation 12:11, 'The final victory of God's people over Satan'.[36]

Nearer home, the students of the Bible Training School had pioneered a work in the Mount Pleasant area, renting a hut for the purpose. It became impossible for the School to afford the rent that was being asked, so Tabernacle Church appointed a group of men to be responsible for the venture, while the students continued their work. A series of missions were held, a prayer meeting and a Sunday school were established, and then a regular evening service.

The mission hut, however, was not really suitable for meetings, and in 1926 Tabernacle ventured to buy the land.[37] During the General Strike of that year the foundations were laid for a new building, most of the labourers being colliers who were not at work. William Evans, JP, provided a horse and cart, and the wages of the workers 'were vouchers for free clothing and two free meals a day'.[38]

The evangelistic van (*Cerbyd yr Efengylydd*) was still travelling. When Griffith Hughes retired in 1919, a suitable successor was found in Matthew Francis from Llanelli. RB gave him his full support.

Like his predecessor, Matthew Francis might spend weeks in one area. During a prolonged visit to the Gwendraeth Valley in Carmarthenshire he decided at one point to stop the van in order to preach and sing, despite the fact that he could see no one around. While preaching, he saw a farmer in the nearby field stopping work to listen to the message, and as he was singing a young girl came out of a house and gave him threepence, thinking he was begging for money.[39] He spent another summer travelling from Cardiff to Pontypridd. He received discouragements in Tongwynlais, but in Pontypridd much encouragement despite initial opposition.[40] This method of Home Mission came to an end in 1924 but was revived later in 1928.

The magazine *Yr Efengylydd* was still being published. Nantlais Williams had joined RB as co-editor. Keri Evans also helped for a brief period, and T. R. Williams (Dafen, Llanelli) joined the two editors in 1926.[41] RB continued to contribute articles, and he took the opportunity to promote overseas mission through the magazine as well as in the church at Tabernacle. The magazine reported news from various missionaries and undertook to receive gifts for their support.

During 1923 and 1924, three of the church members at Tabernacle were set apart for work outside of Wales. Tudor Jones and his wife Lilly (RB's daughter) left for Japan under the auspices of the Japan Evangelistic Band, and Nancy Russell was set apart to work with the Faith Mission of Scotland.

Controversy

RB, the Tabernacle Church and the magazine became involved in controversy during this period. Reports had been received from India referring to the changing doctrinal view of some missionaries, including those working with the Baptist Missionary Society.[42] In 1922 John Thomas, a Baptist minister originally from Maesteg, expressed his concern in a series of articles with such titles as 'The axe at the root' and 'Hunted by heresy'. That same year, Watkin Roberts, who had worked in India and was originally from Caernarfon, addressed the Bible Union, and his address was reported in *The Bible Call*. One of the main targets of their criticism was another Welshman, the BMS missionary George Howells.[43] Both John Thomas and Watkin Roberts contributed articles to *Yr Efengylydd* dealing with these doctrinal deviations.[44]

Cynog Williams (Aberdare) and RB made their views known in *Seren Cymru*, the Welsh Baptist Union weekly newspaper. A subcommittee of the BMS had met in Wales, and its report declared that all doubts concerning the heresy of BMS missionaries were ill-founded; but RB was not satisfied and asked for more information. He wrote a second time to *Seren Cymru,* and others joined in the debate.[45] RB left for America, but kept in touch with what was happening in Wales. He wrote an important article from America in answer to a reply by the Rev. E. Ungoed Thomas on behalf of the BMS.

The latter had commented on the main critics of the BMS, and had referred to four of them personally, namely, Dr Mountain, Rev. R. Wright Hay, Rev. J. I. Macdonald and Mr Watkin Roberts, pointing out that they were not brought up as Baptists. He affirmed that the first three men were baptised but were not committed Baptist Union men, not even Wright Hay and J. I. Macdonald, who had been

BMS missionaries. Ungoed Thomas argued that it was wrong for these four to accuse Baptist missionaries of heresy. The missionaries were orthodox in their beliefs, but some of them would not commit themselves to any theory concerning verbal inspiration, the atonement, or the Second Coming of Christ. This was in keeping with the freedom allowed to Baptists in explaining the truths of the gospel. It was not necessary for anyone to confine himself to one narrow interpretation of truth.[46] Ungoed Thomas then referred to W. R. James, a Baptist missionary who agreed with the four mentioned above. He claimed that all these men had been wrong in criticising George Howells's work, *The Soul of India*, and that in doing so they had been very selective. In closing, Ungoed Thomas quoted from the constitution of the Baptist Union of Wales: 'The Union is constituted of Churches and Closed Communion Cymanfaoedd of the Baptists of Wales'. Such a statement, he wrote, did not include any principle or doctrine.[47]

RB responded with a detailed letter. He argued that Ungoed Thomas had been unfair in his portrayal of the 'critics'. In his article he had not included all the criticisms put forward, and had given the impression that the issue was merely a matter of 'forms and words'. On the contrary, it involved the fundamental truths of the gospel. If it was true that it was merely a matter of forms, words and interpretation, would that not mean that no one in the BMS or Baptist Union denied the deity of Christ, his personal return, or the absolute necessity of atonement for sin? Is the freedom that is allowed to individuals a freedom for them either to accept or deny the physical resurrection of Christ? Baptists in the past had made known their beliefs in a declaration of faith (he could here have referred to the *Baptist Confession* of 1689). He attacked the statement made by Ungoed Thomas that the constitution of the Baptist Union of Wales did not include any principle or doctrine, arguing that there were two dogmatic statements in his quotation from the constitution: one on baptism and another on closed communion. How was it possible to be dogmatic on such issues and yet to be tolerant with respect to the fundamentals of the faith?[48]

Ungoed Thomas's tendency in the controversy was to oversimplify the issues, whereas the tendency with RB was to over-generalise. This was not a time to oversimplify matters, for the 1920s were difficult years for evangelicals. There were divisions within the Church Missionary Society as well as within the BMS. Both at home and abroad, concerns were being expressed with respect to doctrinal developments. On the other hand, while RB was forceful in pointing out deviations from orthodoxy, he did not really deal with the issue of 'fulfilment'. This was the teaching that the deep desires inherent within Hinduism (and within Islam, as argued by Lewis Bevan Jones, another Welshman) were being fulfilled in Christ.[49]

The church at Tabernacle was one with the pastor in this matter. It was resolved that the church would not send money to any society that could not uphold the authority of Scripture. By this they meant a belief that the Bible was the Word of God, God-breathed through men who spoke as they were moved by the Holy Spirit. The church believed that a denial of such a truth contributed to the apostasy 'so prevalent in Christian institutions and work'.[50]

In fact, this whole period was one of controversy for RB. He had become involved in the T. R. Glover controversy, and also, even more personally, in disagreements arising from his plans for forming a new Bible School in Wales. (Both these matters will be discussed later—the T. R. Glover controversy in the chapter dealing with RB's publications (chapter 9), and the heartaches over the establishing of a new Bible school in the next chapter.)

America

During part of 1923, RB was in America on behalf of the Thado-Kookie Mission (of which he was a Council member)[51] and travelling in company with Watkin Roberts, its founder and secretary. The aim of the visit was threefold: to visit American Bible colleges to discover how they operated; to appeal for money to open a Mission College in Calcutta; and to promote interest generally in the Thado-Kookie Mission.[52] One of their contacts in Calcutta was F. Kehl, friend of Jessie Penn-Lewis and also of Pengwern Jones, a Calvinistic Methodist missionary in India.[53]

RB and Catherine arrived in New York with Watkin Roberts on 28 May 1923, having left the children in the care of Sister Sutherland.[54] On their first night there, RB preached at the Eighth Avenue Gospel Mission before the company moved on to Philadelphia. There they met O. R. Palmer, who had spoken at the Ammanford Convention and had arranged the itinerary for their ten-day visit. RB preached at many churches in Philadelphia, including an Episcopal Church. The last two services in which he ministered were held in Berachah, where Palmer was the pastor.[55] Moving on to Chicago, RB's first port of call was the Moody Bible Institute with its thousand students under the presidency of Dr Gray. The MBI course lasted two years, not the usual three, and this was made possible by excluding holidays. RB was to make use of exactly this arrangement later in Wales.[56] At their next stop, in Montrose, RB had the pleasure of again hearing Dr Torrey preach. The latter, like RB himself, always emphasised overseas mission.

At Montrose, RB also attended meetings celebrating the formation of a Ministerial Institute, but could only stay for two days as he was due at Stony Brook, Long Island. Here he enjoyed fellowship with C. G. Trumbull, another who had spoken at the Ammanford Convention.[57] The period 6-17 August was spent in California. During this fortnight, the company travelled through Toledo, Chicago, Denver, Salt Lake City, San Francisco and Los Angeles. In Toledo, RB met D. J. Davies, who had spent some time with the Gospel Van in Wales. He visited the Bible School in Los Angeles and marvelled at the chapel with its perfect acoustics, built to hold a congregation of four thousand. It was a delight also to visit Crockett near San Francisco, where he met a number of people who had emigrated to the States from the Porth area. With them he spent 'a heavenly Sunday'. He felt that some of the Welsh churches where he preached were too near to Hollywood, 'one of the main thrones of Satan'.[58]

RB did not miss the opportunity to visit the Grand Canyon. Everything was breathtaking. It was difficult to grasp the fact that he was looking at a Canyon two hundred miles long, ten to twelve miles wide, and over a mile in depth. Through a telescope it was possible to see further into the Canyon. Every minute brought with it something different to marvel at. He spent eleven hours trying to take in the grandeur of the scenery. His heart whispered the words, 'Great God of wonders'. A day at the Grand Canyon was a day spent with God.[59] RB could appreciate the God of nature as well as the God of grace, knowing that creation and grace were derived from one and the same source.

A brief visit was paid to the southern States. RB preached to an Afro-American congregation, and Mrs Jones recalls the occasion:

There was a little woman in an apron who was clapping hands and praising the Lord. I had a sleeping chair by the door because of the intense heat. There were mosquitoes but they never troubled RB.[60]

New workers, new ventures

When RB returned from America, the first news he heard was that plans were forging ahead for the establishment of a Bible College at Swansea; a college, that is, that would be in direct competition with his own intended Bible School at Porth. This whole episode is a very sorry story and will be discussed in the next chapter. But some good arose from it eventually, in that B. S. Fidler left Swansea and joined RB at Porth. Fidler was appointed assistant minister, and helped RB in the Bible Training School and in mission work.

Further help was by now needed at Tabernacle. D. M. Russell Jones was appointed as a second assistant to RB. Russell Jones was from the Rhondda and had been brought up in a Christian home. It was during a time of family prayers that he had committed himself to God. He attended the Bible Training School from 1922 to 1925, then spent a brief time at Rogerstone, Gwent, before returning upon his appointment to Tabernacle. His testimony was that he spent '3 wonderful years' at Tabernacle.[61] The large church was now regularly crowded in the morning and evening services on a Sunday. Often, chairs had to be brought into the aisles. Every Monday morning, D. M. Russell Jones would meet with RB for prayer—praying for the needs of the church and for revival in Wales.

The church's labours were expanding. Tabernacle adopted Bethany, Ynys-hir, as a daughter-church, and D. M. Russell Jones was appointed and placed there as Pastor-in-charge. A second cause, Penuel, Trehafod, was also adopted, and B. S. Fidler made Pastor-in-charge. The work of building a place of worship at Mount Pleasant had by now been completed, and the new church, Bethlehem, opened its doors at the beginning of 1928. To celebrate the opening, a procession of the Sunday school students of the four churches marched to Bethlehem, and 850 of them were then gathered together for tea. Sidney Watson was the appointed Pastor-in-charge. A particular financial need at the time was a sum to cover the wages of three workers. A gift was received sufficient to pay off this debt.[62]

Tabernacle had its own Home Mission, and would send teams to various districts. One place visited was Tan-y-lan, Pontypridd, known as 'little Russia'.[63] One of the main leaders was Matthew Francis, who had previously travelled with the Gospel Van. Tan-y-lan was a place where many gathered to play cards and listen to jazz music. One Friday evening, many entered the mission tent but continued playing card-games. When the children of the locality came in, they listened quietly. There was much poverty in the area: some of these children were not properly clothed, whilst others walked round without shoes. Friends from Llanelli and Hastings sent gifts of money, making it possible to prepare a good meal for two hundred children.[64]

The appointment of assistant workers enabled RB to travel not only in Wales but also overseas. He visited Riga, Latvia, in 1927 and Canada in 1928.

Riga, Latvia

R. B. Jones was invited to take part in the opening of the Tabernacle Baptist Chapel, Riga. On the day that he started his journey from Cardiff, he saw a placard announcing the death of 'a well-known Cardiff Pastor'.[65] He realised immediately that this referred to Charles Davies, minister of Tabernacle Welsh Baptist Church, Cardiff, a faithful pastor and effective revival leader. After arriving in London, RB made for Spurgeon's Metropolitan

Tabernacle, where he was to meet Charles Philipps who was to accompany him to Riga. They attended a prayer meeting at the Tabernacle that had been arranged as a farewell meeting for them. Then they crossed to Holland and Germany and spent two days in Berlin.[66]

Arrangements had been made in Berlin for the two men to meet Arianwen Jones, a former student of the Bible Training School, together with her fiancé, a man called Propokchuk. The couple were to marry a little later and move to Chicago to work amongst the Russians of that city. The company of four travelled from Berlin to Lithuania. As they approached the border, RB heard a little girl crying 'Maman!' to her mother. The French word sounded in his ears like the Welsh word for mother (*mam*), and for an instant he thought a little Welsh girl was on the train with them.[67]

At long last, tired and having shown their passports on numerous occasions, they arrived at Riga. Here they were welcomed by William Fetler, by Dr McCaig of Spurgeon's College, and by the students and members of the congregation. Fetler's first greeting was *'Croeso! Sut ydach chi?'* ('Welcome! How are you?'). Part of the welcome consisted of a solo from Fetler himself, followed by songs from the student choir.[68]

Riga provided many attractions: the Dom Protestant Cathedral, the Greek Church and the Castle. Everything that might be expected in a large town was to be found there—electric trams, taxis, cinemas and radios. The women wore short skirts to the knee and leather boots with the ankles covered in fur. From the point of view of the kingdom of God, the 'greatest sight' in Riga was William Fetler himself. He went to bed late and rose early, full of energy, 'fresh as a trout'. According to RB, Fetler had 'a good engine', but what RB found most interesting was the steam that kept him going. It was impossible to put him in a class. The man most like him was C. T. Studd.[69]

The great day arrived. The Tabernacle Chapel had been built to hold 800, but on the Saturday morning of the opening it was not finished.[70] It was therefore the adjoining Hall that was officially opened. The first event was a meal prepared for the workers, but Fetler also preached the gospel to them. In the evening the place was full, with a high percentage of men. The ladies had their shawls drawn over their heads (as in Wales before 'bobbed hair' became the fashion). RB, Dr McCaig and Pastor Hoffs from Cassell were the speakers, and during the service use was made of four languages: Russian, Latvian, German and English. RB's sermon was based on John 10:10.[71]

The following day at 8.30 a.m. the first meeting was held in the Revival House. A procession, led by William Fetler and an Inspector of Police who was a member at the Tabernacle, marched from there to the new building. The 10 a.m. meeting continued until 1 p.m. Three meetings a day were held during that week, and the service the following Sunday lasted from 10 in the morning until 3 in the afternoon. RB was very impressed with everything that took place, though he did not appreciate the singing. In his view, Fetler was too ready to make use of his choir, and as a conductor he was no Thomas Beecham! But this was a small matter compared to all that had been achieved under Fetler's ministry.[72]

Other events of note occurred during 1927 and 1928. Towards the end of 1927, William Fetler paid a return visit to Wales. He joined RB, W. S. Jones and others in a convention at Llanelli.[73] While Fetler was in south Wales, his sister was travelling in north Wales, where she was welcomed by Gwynhefin Thomas of Blaenau Ffestiniog, who had been prominent in revival meetings in the Rhondda, and by Dan Jones of Rhyl.[74] RB was still speaking at conventions in Wales and England, and in 1928 he was appointed President of the Bible League.[75] He addressed a number of meetings in different parts of the country, including a service at the Metropolitan Tabernacle. Any deviation from the orthodox view of Scripture he regarded as not only false but dangerous, affecting both faith and practice. During that same year (1928), Geraint Jones, RB's son, was appointed as a further help for his father in the church and the Bible Training Institute.

Another experience that brought RB much pleasure was his visit to Canada to address that country's annual Keswick Convention.[76] His theme for the series was 'The Hidden Heroisms of Faith', and his addresses were subsequently published in 1929. On his first Sunday in Canada he visited Knox Church, Toronto, staying with a married couple originally from Rhos, Wrexham. He was glad when opportunity arose to meet T. T. Shields and Billy Sunday. During the tour, he also went to St Paul, Minnesota, where he once again met with D. J. Davies. At the North-western Bible School, he spent some time with Dr Riley, another person who had spoken in conventions in Wales. And at St Paul's, Chicago, RB was one of three speakers in a series of meetings. It was here that he had his first experience of being recorded for transmission on radio.[77]

By this time (the late 1920s), R. B. Jones was becoming more impatient. At times he reacted rather harshly to weaknesses he perceived in the church at Tabernacle. Being a perfectionist, he always wanted to see marked progress. In 1930 he circulated a Pastoral Letter, 'The Burden of the Valley', calling members to take the church covenant more seriously. The language of the letter was harsh, and it is no surprise that it created division in the church.[78]

116

It is possible that criticisms aired in *The Porth Gazette* influenced RB's attitude. The paper had criticised him regularly, from 1919 onwards, for his 'fundamentalism' and anti-social attitude. During 1928 it had concentrated on his perceived anti-social behaviour: 'Mr Jones has no identity with the town; he ignores every social effort.' Examples given were his refusal to attend the unveiling of a war memorial on a Sunday afternoon, and to send a representative to a meeting of the local branch of the League of Nations.[79]

An event in 1931 posed a different problem for the church. The Baptist Union of Wales was holding its annual meeting in Porth, and Tabernacle had agreed to the use of its vestry for an overflow meeting. The preacher for the meeting was a man called J. Williams Hughes who, much later, became Principal of Bangor Baptist College, north Wales. In accordance with the Constitution of the church, the officers of Tabernacle asked the preacher to assent to the church's doctrinal statement. This in all conscience he could not do, and so the officers barred him from the pulpit.[80] RB was in another chapel at the time, but when called he supported his officers. RB was severely criticised for his action, and even a former student, a staunch supporter of the minister, expressed his disapproval.

7

The Bible Training School and the South Wales Bible Training Institute

On his arrival at Tabernacle Chapel in November 1919, RB faced two demanding tasks. As well as taking up the reins of a new pastorate he had to plan and develop the new teaching ministry that he had commenced only the previous month—the Bible Training School. His various duties placed him under a considerable burden, but by this time he was very experienced in the various aspects of Christian ministry.

Early days

The first session of the Bible Training School for Christian Workers opened on Tuesday 23 September 1919.[1] A small group of ten students—five men and five women—constituted the first intake. Classes were held for four hours each morning from Tuesday to Friday. Some of the men were industrial workers. Gomer Jones was a collier who worked night shifts and studied during the day. It was a tremendous achievement for him to follow the course, for when he entered the Bible Training School he was almost illiterate. From Porth he went to Pagefield College, before proceeding to Bangor and recognition by the Baptist Union of England and Wales.[2] William Jones worked at the Gorseinon foundry. RB urged him to apply for ministry with the Baptist Union, and he later became a leader in the

Brecon Baptist Association. His wife Margaret was also a student at Porth.[3]

Six of the first ten students were considering work overseas. Four of these were a brother and sister from Cross Hands, Carmarthenshire, a woman from the Rhondda, and a young man who was later to marry one of RB's daughters. All four (and the daughter) gained their wish and went overseas. The fifth found work with a Christian Mission at home, while the sixth student went to America. This emphasis on overseas work will be discussed later. RB never lost sight of this aspect of Christian witness.

A former student recalls those early days:

At the time the lectures were held in the Pastor's Vestry, and all in English. There was a small library cupboard of devotional books. In year three we had a uniform. One tutor, W. S. Jones, spoke conversationally and with some irony; he spoke analytically just like a schoolmaster. Mrs W. S. helped then, stressing expression, style, etc. J. R. Morgan, who was not a teacher, dealt with etiquette, etc.[4]

The uniform reflects RB's concern for order and discipline. As the group was very small, supervision was not difficult. By the end of the first session their number had increased to thirteen, and a total of twenty-one were listed as having followed some part or parts of the course during its first year, 1919–20.[5]

J. R. Morgan, mentioned in the quotation above, was not an effective lecturer, but his personal influence upon the students was considerable. The other lecturers were RB himself, W. W. Lewis, Sidney Evans (for a year until, in 1920, he and his wife left for India), J. T. Phillips (Ynyshir) and Keri Evans (Carmarthen).[6] As far as textbooks were concerned, RB in his Bible Synthesis course made use of Gray's *Christian Workers Commentary;* W. W. Lewis chose Moule's *Outline of Christian Doctrine* as a basis for his doctrinal lectures, and the Greek class studied Samuel G. Green's *A Brief Introduction to New Testament Greek.* The aids for Methods of Study were *How to Study the Bible* by Torrey and *The Joy of Bible Study* by Lees.[7]

As a complement to the lectures, the students received a one-page 'Daily Monitor'.[8] This provided information on a variety of topics. Each day a theme was introduced and explained, usually by quotations from various authors. A New Testament word might be discussed, for example. A Daily Monitor page focusing on the word 'interpretation' (2 Peter 1:20) contains a quotation from A. T. Robertson proving that the reference is to the 'source' of Scripture and not to its 'interpretation'. An explanation of the Greek original is then provided. It is surprising how many different authors are quoted: they include R. A. Torrey (on the gifts of the Spirit), Henry Smith, John Owen and many other Puritans on a variety of topics.[9]

At the bottom of most pages were added brief, proverbial quotations. For example: 'One error is a bridge to another' (William Jenkyn); 'The more we give, the more we have' (W. H. Griffith Thomas); 'As every sound is not music, so every sermon is not preaching' (Henry Smith), and 'The peppercorn of praise is all the rent that God looks for' (John Trapp).[10] Such aphorisms are helpful in capturing a truth, and could entice the students to further reading in the works of authors quoted.

Strong emphasis was laid on practical work such as home-visiting, open-air services and tract distribution. Before the end of the first session, two evangelistic campaigns had been held—one in Treharris, led by J. R. Morgan, and another at Pisgah, Loughor, led by Sidney

Evans.[11] A minister who visited the Bible Training School commented on the zeal of the students in taking the gospel to as many places as possible. The other feature, according to the same visitor, was the intense prayer for a better home for the School.[12]

RB took a personal interest in each of the students. He supervised their Sunday activities as well as those in the week.[13] The students would be sent on Sunday preaching engagements and RB would take note of the places that welcomed them and those that were not so welcoming.[14] He also checked how much they received in payment for their services. If they did not receive 2s-6d (12½ p) or more, he would tell them not to return to those churches.[15] During the early years of the Training School, a number of churches refused to make use of the students. This was probably because of RB's aloofness towards the Baptist Union, and because of his criticisms, even of fellow ministers. One student believed it would have been easier for a Freemason to receive a call from some churches than a Porth student.[16] And another student stated: 'rightly or wrongly, we were isolated from all denominations and from district conventions'.[17]

D. J. Williams, who prepared for the School by following its Correspondence Course, had no doubt that 'This £1 course laid the foundation.'[18] He related how on a Monday the students had to give a full account of their activities during the previous week. These activities usually included open-air services as well as Sunday preaching. Open-air meetings were regarded as effective means of evangelism. The students would report on the number of conversions occurring during these meetings. On one occasion, for example, a young woman who had preached in the open air expressed the joy she had experienced because her words had led to the conversion of a young man. The new convert was to enter the Bible Training School, and was later to marry the very woman who had been instrumental in his conversion.[19] Careful preparations were made for these services, especially when a student was about to address an open-air meeting for the first time:

> Before the first student attempt at Open Air work the Principal laid on a prayer and preparation meeting and worked out an exact programme, as always, and also went and stood with us.[20]

Another means of evangelism was the use of 'the Tent' at Trehafod. One student would lead the service, another would pray and a third would give the message.

> Converts were dealt with according to the principles laid down by J. R. Morgan, and also practiced by R. B. Jones who had a set procedure when dealing with enquirers.[21]

During any series of meetings, two students would always be on 'prayer watch'. The Bible Training School students would also assist the Tabernacle members in their evangelistic activities—as during a mission held in 1922, for example.[22] With all this activity, there was little time for relaxation, so RB, though he had little interest in sport himself, would encourage the students to play games in a field at the top of Mount Pleasant. F. S. Coplestone, who later assisted RB at Tabernacle, had played cricket for Wrexham and was responsible for the sports equipment during his stay at the School.[23]

As mentioned in the previous chapter, RB was in America for part of 1923. During this year, and at the beginning of 1924, he had to wrestle with two problems.

The first was the delicate situation arising from the work of the Rev. Rees Howells in establishing another Bible School at Swansea, thus compromising the position of the Porth School; the second was the abiding problem of finding a better home for his School in Porth. Both aspects demand attention.

Swansea and Porth

Rees Howells (1879–1950) and his wife had been deeply influenced by the 1904–5 Revival.[24] They had worked together for a period in Africa, where they experienced a time of revival. In 1920, their mission, the South Africa General Mission, commissioned them to travel throughout Wales reporting on their revival experiences.[25]

Rees Howells was also conscious of the need for a provision to train Christian workers, and after visiting the Moody Bible Institute in America he became more and more convinced of this. He made known his conviction in an address at the Llandrindod Convention of 1922. He also shared his vision with a number of friends and published an article in *Yr Efengylydd* expressing his views. During this period, Rees Howells would refer to 'a School' or 'a School for Wales', but his words were vague and imprecise. Was he referring to developments already under way at Porth, or was he thinking of something entirely different? RB believed that Rees Howells was indeed speaking of Porth. He based this belief on conversations the two of them had held during 1922 and 1923, when they had discussed the various options open to them.[26]

Almost immediately after Rees Howells's return from his visit to America, RB left for the same destination, where he also was very much impressed by the Moody Bible Institute.[27] He still cherished hopes that Rees Howells was supporting the cause of the school at Porth.

Nantlais Williams responded to the call for the establishment of a Bible College and, as a result of Howells's appeal, he used the pages of *Yr Efengylydd* to publicise the latter's fund-raising efforts. He very much hoped that RB, on his return, might be given the wonderful news that two or three thousand pounds had been collected for the Bible School. Nantlais wrote to America, informing RB of developments, and rejoicing that money was being collected for this worthy cause. It seems that he, like RB, had assumed that all concerned were working towards the development and expansion of the existing school at Porth.[28]

However, when RB returned home from America, it was only to be given the startling news that Rees Howells was going ahead with his own plans for opening a new Bible School, to be situated at Swansea. Both RB and his wife recorded their reaction to the news. In a report that she wrote of their American visit, Mrs Jones described how, before leaving the USA, they had met Paget Wilkes, who had told them of Rees Howells's intentions. Then, 'At Cardiff Sister Sutherland told him the story was true and my husband fainted.'[29]

RB revealed his own thoughts in a letter he wrote to Rees Howells:

> I am on my return confronted with an altogether changed plan, together with a fairly organised scheme for an institution on lines utterly distinct from those on which you and myself, from August 1922 to April 1923, worked so harmoniously. Somewhere or other, since we last met, the enemy has crept in in his usual subtle way.[30]

When details of the plans for the new college were revealed, RB disagreed with them profoundly. His first disagreement had to do with the proposed approach of the college to the Welsh religious denominations. Rees

Howells had declared that he would not compete with existing theological colleges. RB could not believe such a statement:

> *Rhwbiais fy llygaid, rhag fy mod yn methu darllen yn iawn.* (I rubbed my eyes in case I was not reading correctly.)[31]

Secondly, Rees Howells was proposing to co-operate with denominational churches, providing students for them as regular pulpit supplies. RB believed that such links with denominational colleges and churches would lead to doctrinal compromise. Thirdly, Rees Howells desired high academic standards; he stated in one letter that the ideal he aimed for was 'consecrated scholarship'. RB was not against an educated ministry, but he did not think it was his work to produce scholars. He preferred the stone of David to the sword of Goliath.[32]

RB asked Rees Howells to state clearly what his view was as to the relationship between the new college-to-be and the School at Porth. Responding by letter, Rees Howells noted that he had been asked many questions since RB's return from America:

> I have been answering questions ever since; you craved for an answer to those questions, 'Whether the Bible College was a Development, a Supplement or a Substitute'. That was answered that it cannot be other than a SUBSTITUTE.[33]

Such a reply can be interpreted in different ways—the dictionary definition of 'substitute' is 'to remedy a deficiency or to make an addition'.

The college in Swansea opened in 1924.[34] The Rev. John Thomas, Myrtle Street, Liverpool, was appointed Principal, with B. S. Fidler, Trelogan, Flintshire, as his co-worker.

Fidler was a schoolmaster who left a £360-a-year job to live in a caravan, with a bicycle as a means of transport.[35] He did not stay long at Swansea. Matters did not turn out as Rees Howells had expected. A serious division took place in the Bible College when students became unhappy at what they described as the 'tyranny' of Rees Howells.[36] Norman Grubb in his account, however, blames the students for their worldliness.[37]

Thus, for example, when one of the students received an Eisteddfod Programme with an invitation to take part in the competitions, John Thomas was asked for his opinion and could see no harm in accepting the invitation. Rees Howells, however, disagreed: to have competed would have been 'worldliness'. John Thomas, B. S. Fidler and most of the students were unsettled, and by October 1925 the Bible College collapsed.[38] John Thomas, Fidler and the students left, and at least one student, F. S. Coplestone, went to Porth. A whole year passed before the Bible College was able to reopen and make a new beginning.

Confirming the work at Porth

B. S. Fidler left Swansea in 1925 and moved to Porth, where he commenced work on 1 January 1926. It was a timely provision, because Seth Joshua, who visited the Bible Training School regularly to lecture, had died in 1925, and Keri Evans had recently failed to deliver his course of lectures because of ill health. T. M. Jeffreys, an English Congregational minister who took his place, only remained for a brief period. RB comments on the provision:

> Last year, Mr B. S. Fidler was appointed resident Tutor. This was a new and responsible venture. Up till then, owing to the fact that all the other Tutors held pastorates, the tuition cost the School nothing; it was

all a labour of love. Mr Fidler, having no other means of livelihood, had to be assigned a certain remuneration. This meant an addition of £208 per annum; in a word, the doubling of our expenditure.[39]

B. S. Fidler was responsible for General Knowledge, Practical Evangelism and New Testament Greek. A few changes were made to the curriculum. Welsh Grammar was introduced, as were voice production and Hebrew for the advanced students.[40]

There were other encouragements during this period. The first open meeting for the School was held in 1925 and became an annual event.[41] Previously, only staff, students and friends had gathered together for such a meeting. Paul Kanamori from Japan spoke at two of these open meetings and attracted large congregations. A union of former students was also formed and proved beneficial for a number of years.[42]

All concerned with the Bible Training School were still searching for a new home. A building fund was launched and soon realised £200. A gift from two of the Cory sisters of Cardiff made it possible to buy Tynycymer Hall, overlooking Porth Square. Their father Richard Cory was also supportive, so much so that it was suggested that the new home should be called 'The Richard Cory Memorial Bible Training Institute'.[43] Another Cardiff businessman covered the cost of turning a stable into a bedroom and a lecture hall.[44] All kinds of gifts were received—not only books and office equipment, but

Among the items received with thanks were a portable organ, a microscope, a hall clock, a washing-machine, a sewing-machine, a set of dictionaries, a lawn roller and an eight-seater Armstrong-Sidley car to take student teams on campaign. Almost every need was sooner or later met by private gifts from people in all walks of life.[45]

The students themselves did most of the practical work required in getting the building ready.

In this way, the Porth Bible Training School became the South Wales Bible Training Institute. From now on it became a residential college. These changes called for an even stricter discipline and a more thorough organisation. RB and his staff oversaw every aspect of the life of the Institute. Particular rules covered the lecture room, the laundry and the cloakroom. Four main principles governed the life of the students: Godliness, Courtesy, Tidiness, and Punctuality. Those guilty of transgressing these principles were rebuked, but if there was consistent rebellion they were asked to leave.[46]

RB had a well-trained, ordered mind, and hated any uncertainty or untidiness. J. R. Morgan was very familiar with his meticulous care for detail:

> One is reminded of the method of the Military General Headquarters, of having portfolios XYZ prepared against conceivable contingency. It was so with RB. His lectures and outlines were planned, typewritten, duplicated, all in their indexed cases, and set on their appropriate shelves in the office. Thus when the Principal had to be away upon the Master's service, the lecture outline and method of work was found available for the occasion.[47]

Enid, one of RB's daughters, would type from dictation, duplicate the letters, bank subscriptions, and help prepare the Daily Monitor.[48] Sister Ellis, who became B. S. Fidler's wife, had charge of the general discipline of the female

Caeharris, Dowlais, where Rhys Bevan Jones was born in 1869. Hebron Chapel can be seen on the right.

Rev. R. B. Jones and (above) Mrs Catherine Jones.

Ainon, Ynys-hir, where R. B. Jones ministered, 1904–1919.
(Photo: Archives and Special Collections, Bangor University)

Ainon, interior.
(Photo: Archives and Special Collections, Bangor University)

R. B. Jones and the officers of Ainon,
Ynys-hir (1913–14).
(Photo: Archives and Special Collections, Bangor University)

Tabernacle, Porth:
R. B. Jones's final
pastorate,
1919–1933.

R. B. Jones with the Sister, elders and deacons of
Tabernacle, 1923.

Superintendent, officers and teachers of the Sunday School,
Tabernacle, during the ministry of R. B. Jones.

The Gospel Van of Yr Efengylydd, c.1912.
(Photo: Archives and Special Collections, Bangor University)

Two close associates of R. B. Jones: Nantlais Williams, Ammanford
(left), and W. S. Jones, Llwynypia.

The tutors and first students of the Bible Training School for Christian Workers, established at Porth in 1919 and later renamed the South Wales Bible Training Institute. Front row, seated: W. Ifor Jones, J. R. Morgan, Sidney Evans, E. Keri Evans, W. S. Jones, W. W. Lewis, R. B. Jones, J. T. Phillips.

Four lecturers at the South Wales Bible Training Institute. Clockwise from top left: D. M. Phillips, B. S. Fidler, J. W. Perry, Geraint Ll. Jones.

The main building of the South Wales Bible Training Institute, Porth.

Student group at the Institute, 1931.

students, while Sister Sutherland gave her time to Tabernacle Church. Both Sisters were directly responsible to RB.

In referring in this way to the strict discipline of the Institute, it is only fair to mention another aspect of RB's character. The man of discipline was also a man of emotion; the man of rules was also a man of song; and the man whom many considered to be aloof could be at one with his students. B. S. Fidler describes one of RB's lectures—the last lecture, in fact, that he delivered at the Institute:

> After giving an account of the Lord Jesus Christ, His office as King, and quoting Heb. 1:6, 'And let all the angels of God worship Him', he burst out in song, 'And crown Him Lord of all'. When he finished the students took up the song and the theological class turned into a meeting for prayer and praise.[49]

The passion of the pulpit could not be kept out of the lecture room.

In 1927, Miss Sutherland left to look after her aged parents, but the next two years brought further additions. The Rev. Sidney Watson was appointed superintendent of the practical work; Mrs A. V. Jones, the Rev. D. M. Phillips (Tylorstown), the Rev. R. T. Gregory (Rhondda) and Geraint Jones, one of RB's sons, joined the staff, and David Evans (Bridgend) visited occasionally.[50] With Geraint Jones's coming, seminars were introduced for the first time, though the other lecturers adhered to straight lecturing.[51] The Correspondence Course was popular, with 240 names on its register. Twenty full-time students were received in 1928, making a total of 42 in all.[52]

Trekking
RB never tired of urging the students to evangelise. Around 1928 a special effort was made, and a number of

treks were arranged for this purpose. Sometimes the students themselves took the initiative. Esther Thomas was anxious to promote mobile evangelism. RB welcomed her zeal but made it clear that no money was available to support her. She found a like-minded friend in Louisa Thornley and together they ventured on the work of evangelism at Llwyncelyn, Porth.[53] Local churches supported them and they were welcomed into many homes in the area. Encouraged, they extended their sphere of labour and travelled to Swansea. They reported on an unbroken series of meetings at Porth, Swansea, Blaengwynfi, Trehafod, Gelli, Llantrisant, Seven Sisters, Ferndale, Clyne, Brynmawr, Ynys-hir and Ton-mawr. RB was Director and Treasurer of this work.[54]

Margaret Francis and May Owen, two Welsh-speaking students, were given the responsibility of travelling with a new version of the Gospel Van. In response to an appeal by RB, William Evans, JP, had provided an old bus,

> which was now fitted with hinged shafts and refitted to R. B. Jones's own patterns (he was a trainee draughtsman). To make possible a quick change from bedsitter to chapel he put in a removable partition, a reversable settee, two foldaway beds and foldable table; concealed cupboards, an alcove for the library case cum pulpit and another for a portable organ.[55]

Before the first trek, RB went with John Thomas (Llandeilo) to choose possible sites for the Gospel Van in the Llandeilo area. On arrival, the gospel witnesses were overwhelmed by the welcome they received. They were showered with gifts, including potatoes, fruit and milk.[56]

Others ventured without a Gospel Van. One group included Ivor Powell, an individualist who would not keep to the arranged programme. On one occasion he could not resist the temptation to challenge a Roman Catholic, for which RB rebuked him because 'I am receiving enough trouble as it is.'[57] Another group accepted a lift to Storey Arms, near Brecon,

> from which we pushed a rubberwheeled cart to Llandovery, Lampeter and Aberaeron. Fred Legge did the preaching and T. J. Davies sang. Nicholas and Lawrence talked to the people and I cooked.[58]

The Irishmen in the Institute led a trek in Northern Ireland:

> We never needed our tent from Belfast to Bushmills, partly because Irishmen were preparing the way. The only hardship was following Campbell's short cuts over wild moors and peat bogs.[59]

The Bible Institute gave plenty of opportunities to the female workers. They went on treks, took Sunday school meetings and sang at various other meetings. After finishing their courses, they could apply to join organisations such as the Liverpool City Mission, the Mildmay Mission, or the Forward Movement of the Presbyterian Church of Wales. Bronwen Hale was converted under RB's ministry, attended the Institute, and on leaving helped with the mission at Trehafod. RB arranged for her to go to a little church in Ynysowen, Treorci, that was on the point of closing. RB went with her on the train to Treorci.

> I demurred at the idea of preaching, yet I knew I had to go. I knew that he had prayed through to God's will for my life (just as Maggie Francis did). At Ynyswen I was helped by students but did my own preaching. Eventually I was ordained by R. B. Jones, not in a

ceremonial way but at a preaching service in the presence of all the students.[60]

Bronwen Hale married A. L. Hughes, and the couple went to India as missionaries under the auspices of the Presbyterian Church of Wales.

Overseas mission

Bronwen Hale was one of many students that went to work overseas. RB was very aware of events in other countries and was anxious to support such missions as the South Africa General Mission, China Inland Mission and Spanish Gospel Mission. Some of the students were to develop into prominent leaders. Glyndwr Davies became one of the leaders of the South Africa General Mission (and, later, of the Dorothea Mission) and afterwards lectured at the Barry Bible College.[61] Mair Davies joined the Baptist Missionary Society and was honoured for her work in India; she received the Kaiser-i-Hind medal at the time of the partition between India and Pakistan.[62] Jack Barkey spent a lifetime with the Hebrew Christian Testimony.[63] During the period from 1919 to 1933 about forty students left for different countries.

As mentioned previously, four of the first intake became missionaries. Two of the four, Sally Evans and Arianwen Jones, went to Latvia and Russia. These were new territories for Welsh missionaries. The link was established through William Fetler, a fellow student of Caradoc Jones, Rhosllannerchrugog, at Spurgeon's College. During their college years both men were influenced by the 1904–5 Revival. These links were strengthened when a Christian centre, called 'Slavanka', was opened in the south of England.[64] A few Welshmen met Fetler there. In 1921 Fetler visited Porth and Llanelli. RB met him then, and subsequently, as mentioned in the previous chapter, RB was to visit Latvia.

During the 1921 convention at Llanelli, nine persons responded to Fetler's call to go overseas. One of these was Sally Evans of Cross Hands, Carmarthenshire, one of the 1919 intake at the Training School. She married D. T. Griffiths from her home area and they left Wales to serve with the Russian Missionary Society. D. T. and Sally Griffiths worked for a brief period with S. K. Hine, author of the English version of the hymn 'How great Thou art'. When at Berlin for a time they met Arianwen Jones, another of the 1919 students, and the three of them, together with Hine, arranged evangelistic services. In Hine's own words,

> In between these long meetings Mr and Mrs Griffiths, Miss Arianwen Jones (a strong Welsh soprano) and I sang as a vigorous quartette at Fetler's meetings in the Wilhelmstrasse YMCA. We had lessons in Russian grammar and diction, invaluable in later years.[65]

The two couples, the Griffithses and the Hines, left the Russian Missionary Society to work under the umbrella of the Open Brethren. Arianwen Jones continued with the Society, and later worked amongst Russians in Chicago.

Not only were students from Porth travelling to Poland and Russia, but believers from these and other countries arrived at Porth. Basil Bura was brought up in a Greek Orthodox family.[66] His mother died when he was young and he worked in a shoe-shop, but had to leave in order to care for his father (his three brothers being in the army). A meeting with evangelical Christians eventually led to his conversion. After two years of military service, he attended the school of Brother Gitling, where he also worked as a gardener. During this time he saved enough money to travel to Wales in 1927.[67]

George Urban was one of William Fetler's assistants in Riga, Latvia. He had graduated at Moscow and had become a judge, but after his conversion he committed himself to Christian work. He was supported during his stay at the Institute by the Tabernacle Young People's Guild.[68] Jacob Vagar was a schoolteacher. During his years as a teacher, and afterwards when in the army, he was confused emotionally. He could see no purpose in life and at one time considered suicide. Then, when searching for something in a trunk, Vagar came across a New Testament, and the reading of it led to his conversion.[69] Joseph Schwartz was a converted Jew, and at first William Fetler thought that the new convert was too immature to enter his Bible College. Schwartz continued to preach, however, and made such progress that Fetler accepted him for training. After a brief period of study, Schwartz crossed to Porth to be with RB.[70]

Another overseas student was Ferrazine from Nogent sur Marne, Paris—a Bible School founded by Reuben Saillens. After his time at Porth, Ferazzine went as a missionary to Haiti.[71] One student came from Damascus. RB obtained financial help for him, and the student presented to Mrs Jones embroidered table-mats made by his congregation at home.[72]

Visitors to Porth

Through the Monthly Meetings and Annual Meetings of the Institute, it was possible to hear a variety of speakers from far afield. This must have enriched the lives of the students. Speakers as different as Christabel Pankhurst, the suffragette and evangelist, Dr Cynddylan Jones, Dr W. B. Riley, the American fundamentalist leader, Dr Martyn

Lloyd-Jones, and the Revs John McNeill and Gresham Machen, contributed to the success of these meetings.

Students would remember visiting speakers for different reasons. One young man remembered the visit of Sadhu Sundar Singh. During the service, the young man became convinced that God was calling him to Christian service. Immediately after the meeting he went to RB, who prayed with him and was assured that he was in the path of God's will. He entered the Bible Training School, and after his training became a faithful pastor and a respected JP at Tenby.[73]

The visit of T. T. Shields, Canada, was remembered for a different reason. During one of his addresses he rebuked the churches for their slackness—they promised so much and fulfilled so little. Many were humbled. The students arranged a prayer meeting to seek renewal personally and revival in Wales:

> After hours on their knees praying for revival, R. B. Jones came in and quietly suggested they should go to bed. One student accused him of hindering revival that night. He was really grieved.[74]

This episode provides just one example of RB's spiritual discernment.

Visitors often commented after spending time at the Institute. In 1935, William Fetler gratefully recalled his visit:

> I shall never forget in Porth, in R. B. Jones' Church, when the message was given and the invitation to volunteer, how they came and knelt at the altar. The first missionary from Wales to Russia was Sister Arianwen Jones. She is still working with the Russian people.[75]

Fetler was speaking at the time at the Annual Convention of the Apostolic Church at Pen-y-groes, Carmarthenshire.

Two outstanding men from America (both lecturers at Princeton Seminary at the times of their visits and both afterwards founder-members of Westminster Seminary) delivered lectures at the Institute. In his address, R. Dick Wilson encouraged the students, declaring with great passion that he would use his last breath to stand for the Word of God and to defy its critics.[76] J. Gresham Machen wrote a personal account of his first visit to Porth. He visited Tynycymer Hall, and as he spoke the 'ejaculations' came freely, but they were not forced. The singing was 'fine':

And then after enjoying the beautiful pastoral scene in the garden one experiences a shock observing the hideousness all round in the great mountains of slag above, the ugly town immediately beneath. It seemed like a tragedy. I could hardly shake off the pathos of it.[77]

This first visit of Machen's coincided with a difficult period economically for the Welsh valleys on account of the coal strike of 1926 and France's embargo on British coal. Machen returned in 1932 and spoke on 'Christian scholarship', a series of lectures that he had delivered at Caxton Hall, Westminster. These addresses were later published under the title *What is Christianity?*

8
Main doctrinal themes

In his published works, as in his preaching ministry, RB concentrated on three main themes: Sanctification, Revival and the Second Coming of Christ. We shall consider his main emphases for each topic in turn.

Sanctification

RB's views on sanctification are most clearly expressed in his book, *The Gospel for the Believer (A study of Romans 5–8)*, published in 1933.[1] His starting point is the 'Gospel of God' (Romans 1:1). In chapters 1 to 4 Paul explains how God had dealt with man's sin and had provided the means of justification. Chapter 5 then begins with 'justification', and chapter 8 brings it to an end with 'glorification'. Chapters 1–4 are linked to the Old Testament, but chapters 5–8 are 'utterly new'.[2]

The theme of chapter 5 is deliverance, 'deliverance from death to life'. 'Enemies' are reconciled to God, are justified, and are led on to a 'hope' that is nourished by 'tribulation'. The ground of hope is the 'love of God shed abroad in our hearts by the Holy Ghost which is given unto us'. RB deals rather briefly with the section from verse 12 to verse 21, concentrating on verses 13-14 and 20-21. The organic unity of the race explains the possibility of the imputation of the sin of one to all, and of the righteousness of one to many.[3]

The deliverance discussed in chapter 6 is that of deliverance from 'sin to righteousness'. The question, 'Shall we

137

sin that grace may abound?' is answered by noting that grace is an enemy of sin. Grace produces holiness: 'Deliverance from sin's guilt and penalty is possible only by the death of Another for us, but deliverance from the thraldom of sin depends upon our death with Him.'[4] For some time, RB was uncertain as to the meaning of the phrase 'the old man', and how it was related to 'the flesh'. He became convinced that 'the flesh' stands for 'the old personality' and has to be put to death. It is the new man that is able to die to sin. The 'old man' on the other hand has been crucified. The dying to 'Sin', not sins, is 'complete in one act'.[5]

Another difficult question is the meaning of the references to 'body' in chapter 6. The 'old man' was crucified so that 'the body of sin' might be 'surrendered impotent and inoperative'. The body of every Christian is a 'body of sin'. It is true that 'the old man' has been crucified with Christ and that new life has been given to him, but he has to deal with the 'body of sin'. In discussing Romans 6:6, RB claims:

> It seems to me that Paul uses it in the sense as referring to this sinful body—the 'mortal body' of verse 12 with its desires.[6]

This is also his view of the meaning of the phrase 'mortal bodies' in Romans 8:11. Similarly, when referring to Paul's exhortation not to yield our 'members' to unrighteousness, he notes that the exhortation can only be understood if the reference is to the actual members of our mortal bodies.

RB is certainly correct in claiming that 'body' in Romans 5–8 refers to our mortal, physical bodies. But there are two dangers with this exposition that must be avoided. Although correct in distinguishing between 'the old man' and 'the body of sin', RB emphasises the point to such an extent that his view could be taken as meaning that the body, in and of itself, is sinful. He is also too ready to describe man's being as made of separate, distinguishable parts. He speaks of sin as being delivered from 'the will' and 'the spirit', and making the body its stronghold. RB is again correct in saying that sin makes the body its stronghold, but in distinguishing so distinctly between one 'part' of man's being and another, he loses sight of the unity of the human body and the human spirit. They are to be distinguished, but not separated as in RB's exposition.

As he proceeds to chapter 7, RB is very conscious that he should do so with 'a humble heart of a child'.[7] He is aware that there are different opinions with respect to the chapter and he does not wish to be dogmatic. He believes that 'The chief limiting verses are 4, 7 and 14.' The theme is deliverance from 'Law' in order to be under 'grace'. The believer is not under the Law, because Law's condemnation has been removed, and the Law cannot produce holiness. Grace, however, brings the sinner into such a state of holiness.[8]

Who is described in this chapter? Is it the believer or the unbeliever? RB makes the very helpful point: 'As a general principle, remember that it is not the habit of Scripture to give much time or space to unregenerate experience.'[9] He argues that this chapter must be linked with Romans 8:1. Those persons mentioned in chapter 7 are the same as those whom Paul describes as 'in Christ' in Romans 8:1. Those in Christ are not 'in the flesh', but it is possible for them to 'walk after the flesh'. The Law sets 'in motion' the 'Sin-principle', and consequently there is a battle between spirit and flesh. It is this warfare that Paul is dealing with in chapter 7. It is the warfare of the believer.[10]

139

Attention is given to the various uses of 'I' in the chapter: 'There is only one I in the unregenerate.'[11] RB believes that Paul is looking back over his past life in verses 7-14, but from verse 14 his use of the word 'I' might refer, depending on the context, to his 'whole being', to the 'new man', or to the 'flesh' that still clings to the believer. He elaborates on this point when expounding verse 15:

> That which I (the flesh) do, I (the new man) allow not; for what I (the new man) would, that I (Paul as a whole) do not; but what I (the new man) hate, that do I (the flesh).

The greatest wonder of all for RB is that it is possible to say with Paul: 'Now then it is no more I that do it, but sin that dwelleth in me.' He relates Paul's teaching to that of John, who states, on the one hand, 'he that is born of God cannot sin', and on the other hand, 'If we say that we have no sin, we deceive ourselves.'[12] The new man cannot sin, but the flesh still troubles him.

According to RB, Romans chapter 8 is 'one of the grandest chapters in the Bible'.[13] He believes that the two main themes of the chapter are the work of the Holy Spirit in the life of the believer, and the consummation of all things to the glory of God. The only previous reference in the letter to the Holy Spirit is found in Romans 5:5, but in chapter 8 he has a central place. He is: (1) 'The Spirit'; (2) 'The Spirit of life in Christ Jesus'; (3) 'The Spirit of God'; (4) 'The Spirit of Christ', and (5) 'The Spirit of him that raised up Jesus from the dead'.[14] RB comments briefly on each reference to the Holy Spirit in the chapter, namely, as 'the Quickener of the natural body'; 'the Spirit of Resurrection'; 'the Spirit of Victory'; 'the Spirit of Obedience'; 'the Spirit of Hope'; 'the Spirit of Assurance';

'the Spirit of Sympathy', and 'the Spirit of Prayer'. Although he had referred to the important theme of the 'consummation of all things', he does not in fact deal with that aspect.[15]

In discussing the 'quickening of the body' (verse 11) RB emphasises the present as well as the future. The Spirit presently quickens the body of the believer. The believer must yield himself wholly to God, and in yielding will receive 'the quickening specially given by the Holy Spirit'. Paul had such an experience, as recorded in 2 Corinthians 12. God gives such experiences to those who trust him.

> He cannot trust everybody with it, but those whom he trusts, he lets them have that wonderful experience. In a measure everyone of us knows the quickening of the mortal body by the Holy Spirit.[16]

It cannot be denied that God gives physical strength, and that he can give it in an exceptional way, but RB is claiming that some experiences come to some believers only, and that the receiving of these experiences depends on the degree of trust. This suggests that there are two classes of believers—one on a higher plane than the other. R. B. Jones was too ready to divide Christians into such classes. It is something that he does, not only in dealing with the Christian life, but also in the context of the Second Coming of Christ, as will be discussed later.

Believers are 'in Christ' (Romans 8:1), and RB elaborates on this theme in his work, *Christ Our Life* (1934). The whole life of the Christian must be Christ-centred, for spiritual life comes to the branches only from the vine. The husbandman grafts the branches into the vine, and uses the pruning knife in his care for the new life.[17] The believer has been made free to live the new life,[18] and this life is a gift

from God (John 10:10).[19] Life's ideal is found in Romans
8:29, where Paul is stating that it is God's purpose to con-
form believers to 'the image of his Son'. RB relates this
verse to Genesis 1:29—the record that God created man in
his own image.[20] That image of God is to be restored in
Christ. As the new life is lived out, its characteristics
become evident—trust, obedience, and discipline.[21] There
must be, however, a definite commitment—'the sanctification which is an act once and for all'—before the believer
can live the full Christian life.[22]

This 'once and for all act' enables the believer to live
'in Christ' because he is crucified with Christ. It is a life of
'apartness', and the Holy Spirit continually strengthens the
believer in it. He takes control of the whole life of the
believer, but does so in a particular order. RB emphasised
the primacy of the human spirit: 'The holiest in the human
temple is the spirit.' With the Holy Spirit in control, the
believer experiences 'entire sanctification': 'While life has
its seat in the spirit, it finds its expression by means of the
soul and the body.'[23] The whole man lives in the Spirit.

In order to express the same truth, RB adopts another
image, saying that the life of the risen Saviour is lived out
in the Christian. He refers to Romans 5:10 and insists that
the reference is to the life of the risen Saviour and not to
his earthly ministry. 'Being justified by his blood we shall
be saved by his life.'[24] The 'proprietor' is the 'intercessor'.
The one who laid himself on the altar has entered the holy
of holies. The believer can also look to the future with a
living hope. RB stresses the future aspect of salvation, and
quotes 2 Corinthians 7:10, Philippians 1:19 and 3:20, Titus
2:11-13, Hebrews 9:28 and 1 Peter 1:5. He believed that
this aspect of Christian truth was being neglected generally. It is the Holy Spirit who is at work in the life of the
Christian. He is the one who sustains Christ's life in the

believer. Consequently, the believer can overcome in the power of the Spirit and look to the future with a living hope.[25] The Spirit sustains the 'life within' (John 20:22).[26] Life is the believer's goal, and life is his strength.[27]

Such teaching establishes a living relationship between the believer and Christ. There are many positive aspects to it: life in Christ is that of holiness; the future aspect of salvation is emphasised; and as RB so insistently stresses, life in Christ cannot be lived without the power of the Holy Spirit. Some of his statements, however, are open to criticism. RB grapples with the problem of the relationship between God's sovereignty and man's responsibility. When dealing with the receiving of the Spirit he claims: 'While there is necessarily a real co-operation on the part of the human, the gift itself is not human in any sense, nor is the power by which it is received merely human.'[28] He also claims, as when writing of the pruning work of the husbandman, 'He can only do it with your consent.'[29] With care, it is possible to reconcile and justify these statements, but it would be difficult to justify his words when he makes similar statements in the context of the believer's initial salvation. In this context, his comments confuse responsibility and ability, and detract from the effectual call of God.

In both *The Gospel for the Believer* and *Christ Our Life*, RB teaches a tripartite view of man. The Holy Spirit controls the spirit of the believer, and consequently can control body and soul. Related to this theme is RB's claim that a believer can receive the Spirit without being conscious of having received him. He illustrates his statement thus: a man places a bank note into the pocket of a friend, who is unaware of what is happening. He puts his hand into his pocket and discovers the bank note. It is up to him to decide whether he will bank it or not.[30] It is not an illustration that reveals RB at his best.

The aspect of faith in the life of the believer is dealt with in *Hidden Heroisms of Faith* (Philadelphia, 1928; Porth, 1929). These addresses, which are based on Hebrews 11:32-34, deal with three themes: 'Wrought righteousness'; 'Obtaining the promises'; 'Out of weakness made strong'. It is biblical and more devotional than RB's other works and includes a very helpful character study of Moses.

Sanctification involves consecration, and consecration means being totally committed to God, totally yielded to him. In the Annual Convention at Ammanford in 1925, RB delivered his addresses on *'Arian ei Arglwydd'* ('His Lord's Money'). These were published in Welsh that same year and under the same title. He realised that this was not a popular subject, and one very rarely, if ever, discussed at conventions for the deepening of spiritual life. He was convinced, however, that the right attitude to money was an essential aspect of the life of holiness. Withholding money that belonged to God displeased him, and the displeasure would deprive his people of greater blessing, including the blessing of revival.[31] The Bible contains considerable teaching on the believer's use of money: Matthew 6:19-34; Mark 12:41; Romans 12:8,13; 2 Corinthians 8–9; Ephesians 4:28, for example.[32] RB believed that spiritual blessings should be paid for by meeting the material needs of others. Such giving leads to greater blessings. The believer must pray the prayer of faith, but he must also give that he might receive. Malachi 3:10 presents a challenge to every believer:

'Bring the whole tithe into the storehouse, that there may be food in my house. Test me in this', says the Lord Almighty, 'and see if I will not throw open the floodgates of heaven and pour out such blessing that you will not have room enough for it.'

RB was convinced that a willing response from God's people would please God and would meet the needs of the poor at home and the work of mission overseas.[33] In the second chapter, 'The Example', RB discusses the system of tithing in the Old Testament. This system was introduced suddenly in Genesis 14:18-24 (see also Hebrews 7:1,2) and further detail was added, ensuring that provision was made for the needy, the widow, the orphan and the stranger.[34] RB describes the tithes of the Old Testament according to the instruction given in Deuteronomy 12:17-19; 14:28-29, and Malachi 3:10. As well as tithing, we read of voluntary gifts.[35] God legislated with respect to the Sabbath and also with respect to the act of giving, and both contexts are related to worship. To give willingly is an act of worship.

In chapter 3, RB deals with the pattern of giving, basing his words on 1 Corinthians 16:2. The believer should be happy to give because the life of Christ, the great giver, is being lived in and through him. The giving of the Jew in the Old Testament should shame those living under the New Covenant. Christians are under grace and their lives should reflect that grace in all aspects of life, including their giving. RB emphasises that it would be better to tithe, as in Old Testament times, than to give unworthily.[36] There is a freedom in the New Testament in this, as in other contexts, but a freedom in the spirit and not in the flesh. There is both freedom and order, as is evident from 1 Corinthians 16:1,2. Grace gives, but grace also demands, and it demands more than the Law.[37]

RB was aware that he might be giving the impression that he was recommending tithing, and even the impression that tithing was obligatory for the church. He himself had practised tithing in the past, but no one 'had a warrant to legislate to his fellow believers. The truth is the New Testament legislates very little in this matter.'[38]

Next, in chapter 4, he discusses the spirit of giving on the basis of John 4:24. A proper spirit will be present when the believer remembers that he is giving to God, and that he has been bought with a price. A believer will therefore give gratefully and cheerfully and, if need be, sacrificially. Giving should never be a burden; the believer should give gladly. He refers to 1 Corinthians 9:17, 'for God loveth a cheerful giver', and notes that the original Greek word for 'cheerful' is the basis for the English word 'hilarious'. The believer should accompany his giving with the same feeling of exultation that is felt during revival times, or with the same spirit of joyful hallelujahs as should accompany our prayers.[39]

RB's thinking, as expressed in *His Lord's Money*, was a valuable contribution and was presented biblically and without dogmatism. It was much needed in evangelical circles in those days, as the believer's use of money was a very neglected subject at the time.

The Holy Spirit and Revival

According to R. B. Jones, the doctrine of the Holy Trinity is an essential Christian doctrine. His teaching portrayed the Holy Spirit as a personal being, in a Trinitarian context. To confirm his argument, he made use of the relevant passages in John, chapters 14–15. The Spirit is the third Person of the Godhead, co-equal with the Father and with the Son. He is the one who works grace in the life of the individual believer and the one who blesses the church, in ordinary times and in times of revival. When dealing both with the believer and with revival, RB is more concerned with the fruits of the Spirit than with the gifts of the Spirit. In all his writings, he never loses sight of the concept of revival.[40]

His book *Rent Heavens* (1931) is not a doctrinal study of revival, nor is it, strictly speaking, a history of the

1904–5 Revival. While of great help in understanding its history, it is essentially a personal account, supplying many helpful insights into the origin and development of the movement. Thus it is an important study by a man who was one of the revival's main leaders.

Revival is an extraordinary work of God, and RB describes it as 'unusual' and as the 'strange work of God' because it is so full of mystery.[41] It is from above and never comes from below. It is impossible to work up a true revival. God himself must send the Holy Spirit in great power. Revival stirs the church and the whole community; consequently, it inevitably affects the emotions. This is an essential aspect of revival, though RB was very wary of 'uncontrolled spasms of emotion'.[42] The Holy Spirit quickens life and gives unusual experiences, but he is essentially a Spirit of order.

There was a time, before 1904, when RB believed that revival would come without much emotion, but as a strong moral emphasis. The experience at Llandrindod in 1903 and at early revival events, however, changed his mind completely:

> Since then he has learned that when the Holy Spirit is doing His 'strange work' there is nothing so unreliable a guide as our poor human wisdom, and that those who fear being deemed as 'full of new wine' had better give the Pentecosts and Revivals as wide a berth as possible.[43]

A 'barrage of ice' hampered the progress of the Revival in many places, and RB was very critical of those who 'slandered' the work of God: 'To attribute to carnal emotion what was manifestly the work of the Holy Ghost can hardly be less than blasphemy.'[44] He made use of quotations by Bishop Moule, by the vicar of Rhos, and by Evan

Roberts, to buttress his argument with respect to the place of emotion in revival.

RB describes this 'strange work' of God in many ways. It is 'an outburst of the Spirit'; the Spirit is 'poured out'; it is 'the coming down of God'.[45] Crusades or missions cannot be described in this way, because they are organised by man, have a set pattern and are controlled by the clock. It is true, however, that God can turn a mission into revival. In the 1904–5 Revival, 'Clocks were completely out of action.'[46] This was so because God was manifesting himself. People were living in the spiritual world, beyond time. God was present. There was a 'felt presence of God':

> Felt, of course, in the Revival gatherings, it was by no means confined to them; it was also felt in the homes, on the streets, in the mines and factories, in the schools, yea, and even in the theatres and drinking-saloons. The strange result was that wherever people gathered became a place of awe, and places of amusement and carousal were practically emptied.[47]

The presence of God led to deep conviction of sin, but as the Holy Spirit revealed the crucified Saviour, grief for sin was turned into spontaneous praise, prayer and singing. Spontaneity was a marked feature of revival meetings.

The source of revival is God himself, but he does use means. The Spirit of God moves mightily. He might come directly upon a people, or he might use means, in particular the means of the word of God. RB deplored the fact that many ministers did not preach regularly during the 1904–5 Revival. He was not happy with the way that Evan Roberts had led the work. The 'mystical strain' in Evan Roberts's experience was foreign to the Baptist preacher, and he judged that the revivalist became 'a spectacle rather than a prophet'.[48] Jessie Penn-Lewis asked RB's opinion of Evan Roberts's meetings in Liverpool. In reply, RB acknowledged the good that Evan Roberts had done, and that what he said was usually quite valuable, including the four points he had introduced during the first week in Loughor. Evan Roberts believed that, for revivals to occur, believers must:

1. confess before God every sin in their past lives that has not been confessed;
2. remove anything that is doubtful in their lives;
3. surrender totally, and say and do everything that the Spirit told them;
4. make a public confession of Christ.

But alongside his commendation, RB had reservations.

> I do not know what to say. Everywhere he has been there seems to be a deeper work needed that (*sic*) what he is doing. What an amazing man he himself is! He seems to have no parallel. I cannot recall among all God's great messengers anyone who adopted methods like his. A prophet is surely greater than an actor (I do not of course use the word 'actor' in any unworthy sense). A man with a message is undoubtedly of greater value than one whose chief power seems to be an indefinable mystical hypnotism. I fear he is going off God's lines. After reading of the detection of all kinds of hindrances at his meetings and his publication of the same, one finds himself asking, *Qui homo?*[49]

Neither W. S. Jones nor RB spoke at any length of their own spiritual experiences.

R. B. Jones stressed that the Word of God must have its rightful place:

The Word of God is not only pure, it is also purifying. Its giving forth, whether in reading, preaching, or teaching, has a vital effect upon a meeting's atmosphere and success, for it lays an effectual check upon any elements therein that may be carnal. Others of the Revival's leaders, men of less fame but hardly of less influence, did not, glad to record, give up preaching and teaching of the Word.[50]

And the Word, according to RB, should first of all be applied to the Church, and then through the Church to those outside. This was RB's own method during the Revival and during the whole of his ministry.

In this context of the means of revival, RB deals with the link between Keswick, Llandrindod, and the 1904–5 Revival. He claimed that there was a very close link indeed, and could not understand why 'the nurse did not seem to welcome as heartily as might be expected what was in a large measure her child'.[51] While deploring the lack of preaching in the ministry of Evan Roberts, his four points were, according to RB, 'essentially the message emphasized at Spiritual Conventions such as Keswick and Llandrindod'.[52] Evan Roberts presented the four points as conditions, and RB seems to do so as well. There tends to be a tension, therefore, in their understanding of the sovereign act of God in revival, and the fulfilling of conditions before God will act. It is possible that RB would not acknowledge any such tension, arguing that it is God who gives the Spirit so as to enable believers to fulfil the conditions. He does not clearly distinguish between 'preparation' and 'condition'.

It is strange that RB does not deal with the topic of 'the Baptism of the Spirit' in *Rent Heavens*. He laid much emphasis on it in his teaching. He believed that it was a crisis experience separate from conversion. Every believer should seek it. That is, it should be an experience that believers should look for, irrespective of revival. On the other hand, RB believed that it was an experience linked with revival. He describes it as the condition of revival; he goes so far as to say that the baptism is revival. Here again there are tensions inherent in his teaching.

Three other points must be mentioned. Firstly, RB believed that revival, by definition, lasts only for a short time.[53] Secondly, he emphasised that, with respect to revival, the most important consideration is the measure of its lasting fruit.[54] And lastly, RB connected his views on revival to his understanding of dispensational teaching.[55] The 1904–5 Revival gave an important place to Christ's Second Coming, and this is an emphasis not found in other revivals. According to RB, this truth might be pointing to the fact that they were living in the last days. The revival was preparing his people for that day. RB, writing in 1930, believed firmly in the imminence of the Second Coming.

The Second Coming of the Lord Jesus Christ

The main source for RB's teaching on the Second Coming is his book, *Yr Ail-Ddyfodiad yng Ngoleuni'r Epistolau at y Thesaloniaid* (The Second Coming in the Light of the Epistles to the Thessalonians, 1919). He was aware that he was dealing with an unpopular doctrine, and one that was unacceptable to most of the theologians of his day. In his introduction he quotes some of these authors, without actually naming them, and deals with three main points. Firstly, the claim was being made that John's Gospel presents the coming of Christ in 'spiritual' terms and does not teach a literal, physical coming of Christ. RB acknowledges that there is a 'spiritual' emphasis in the Gospel, but he also refers to other passages (1:51; 14:3; 21:22) and makes the point that John's Epistles should be included in the discussion as well.[56] Secondly, and bound up with this claim, is the belief that Christ's Coming was in the person of the Holy Spirit on the Day of Pentecost. If this were the case, RB argues, then it was strange, to say the least, that Paul and others were still expecting a literal coming after the Day of Pentecost. They knew of that day and of what then occurred. But, as far as they were concerned, Pentecost and the Second Coming were two separate events—one related to the Holy Spirit, and the other to Christ. RB refers to Acts 1:10-11 to confirm his argument, contrasting these verses that refer to Christ with verse 8 in the same chapter with its reference to the Holy Spirit.[57]

Some of the critics believed that Paul was mistaken regarding the Second Coming. They argued that in his early days he believed in an imminent Coming, but that Christ did not return and so Paul had to adjust his thinking accordingly. In his response to this third point, RB lists Scripture passages from the earliest of Paul's letters to his last. Some of the the references point to an imminent coming, but there are others that point to a delayed coming. Both sets of Scriptures must be considered together. They must also be interpreted in relation to the nature of Christ's kingdom. Christ is continually bringing his kingdom into being. Similarly, in Matthew 16:27 there are references to a future day of judgement and, in verse 28, a reference to an imminent coming of Christ at his resurrection. Through the ministry of the Church the kingdom is both presently coming into being and, in the future, will be fully brought in at its consummation.[58]

In expounding his views, RB could write biblically and also dogmatically. In his biblical studies he makes use of the Greek version; he appeals to the Revised (1885) and Inter-Linear (1906) versions; he includes translations from

Weymouth and Ellicott, and he refers to the expositors Denney and Findlay.[59]

When he writes more dogmatically, he is a typical representative of the evangelical theology of the period, in that he refers to the teaching of C. I. Scofield[60] and deals with the Second Coming from a premillennial point of view. He argues for seven dispensations: (1) The Dispensation of Innocence. (2) The Noahic Economy. (3) The Dispensation of Civil Government. (4) The Dispensation of Patriarchal Rule. (5) The Mosaic Law. (6) Grace. (7) The Millennial Reign. During the period of Patriarchal Rule, God through Abraham concentrated his purpose on one people—the one nation of Israel. It is essential therefore, argues RB, to distinguish between biblical references to Israel and those to the Church. God's promises to Israel will be fulfilled during the millennial reign, whereas the Church was brought in, in the time of the Book of Acts, to be God's witness during the present period of the rejection of Israel.[61]

There was no Church in the Old Testament. It was born with the giving of the Holy Spirit on the Day of Pentecost. On that day, the promises of the Old Testament, especially Joel 2, were only partially realised, and will be completely fulfilled in the millennium period with the restoration of Israel. Israel will return to her land, Christ will set up his kingdom, and Israel and the Church will together be the instruments of his government—Israel on earth and the Church in heaven.[62] In an article on the subject, RB bases his arguments on verses from chapters 2, 3 and 7 of the Book of Daniel. The phrase 'the saints' is to be understood as referring to Israel, and 'the kingdom' will be given to her. The four kingdoms (depicted by the image of Daniel 2) will be crushed by the little stone: that is, Christ will return and restore the kingdom to the saints.[63]

The first event of the Second Coming is described in 1 Thessalonians 4:16-17. The coming will be the *'parousia'*, signifying the presence of a person who intends to remain. The dead in Christ will be raised to meet with Christ in the air. It will be, according to RB, a 'triumphant' and 'silent rapture'. No one will realise what has happened because of the suddenness of the event and because believers will be taken to be with Christ. After a brief period, Christ will appear personally and visibly. In another article, RB explains this period to be a time of seven years. During that brief time, the 'day of the Lord' will be revealed, the day of God's wrath upon the enemies of Christ and his people. Satan will be bound, after a brief period of rebellion, and the way will then be opened for fruitful evangelism.[64] Christ will reign for a thousand years, and will rule with his people. At the end of the thousand years Christ will appear as judge, to judge all unbelievers. Having accomplished his work, Christ will usher in a new heaven and a new earth.

RB adopts a literal interpretation of the thousand years. Even if he were correct, which is doubtful, there remain many problems with such an interpretation. To whom does the 144,000 of Revelation 7 refer? What is the significance of the silence in heaven for half an hour? Bound up with this interpretation is his insistence that any reference to 'Israel' has the same meaning every time in the New Testament. But is this truly the case? Is it true of references in Romans 9:6 and Ephesians 2:12? One consequence of his interpretation is that RB applies the blessings of Abraham to Israel, but only partially to the Church. But all the blessings of Abraham and of David are to be applied to the Church, in Christ. The promise to Abraham was a blessing to all the families of the earth (Genesis 15 and 17). The 'sure mercies of David' are in Christ (Acts 13:32-34).

Converted Jews and Gentiles alike belong to 'the commonwealth of Israel' (Ephesians 2:11-19), and they all, by faith, are the seed of Abraham (Galatians 3:29) and the 'Israel of God' (Galatians 6:16). There is no justification for separating the Church and Israel, as RB does in his presentation of the doctrine.

Different shades of meaning may be found in terms like '*parousia*', '*epiphaneia*', '*apocalupsis*', and '*phanerosis*', but they all convey aspects of the same event. RB argues that '*parousia*' refers to the Second Coming as related to the saints.[65] But this is not the case in Matthew 24:37-39, nor in the following paragraph in that chapter, where Christ deals with the faithful and unfaithful servants. If RB was right in claiming that the 'day of the Lord' will occur between the silent and the actual coming of Christ, then there is a difficulty with 2 Thessalonians 2:1-4. Paul is there describing events that will occur before Christ's coming, but to describe them he uses terms like the 'coming', or the 'day of the Lord', which is hardly consistent. Furthermore, he states that before 'that day' comes there must be a 'falling away', and the time when the 'man of sin will be revealed'.

There are also passages of Scripture that refer clearly to the Second Coming as being one event but with different aspects. When the Lord Jesus will be revealed, God will recompense believers and unbelievers (2 Thessalonians 1:7-10). He will judge the 'quick and the dead at his appearing and his kingdom' (2 Timothy 4:1; Matthew 25).

Despite these exegetical weaknesses, however, RB is to be commended for drawing attention to the doctrine of Christ's Second Coming. He safeguarded an important scriptural truth that was being attacked by many in his day. The doctrine enables believers to view history as salvation history, and it gives them a living hope for the future. RB is also very strong on the practical implications of the truth of the Second Coming. Believers should be awake, should discipline themselves, live morally, and grow in spiritual grace. RB emphasises that in the Letters to the Thessalonians the parallel theme to that of 'the Coming', is 'holiness'.[66]

9
Defence and attack

IN RB's eyes, Modernism was seen as a threat to the orthodox Christian faith. He had protested against its emergence in the Baptist Missionary Society and was outspoken in condemning it in the colleges and pulpits of Wales. The appointment of T. R. Glover as Vice-president of the Baptist Union grieved both RB and the church at Tabernacle.

T. R. Glover had made known his beliefs in *The Jesus of History* (1917) and in a series of articles in the *Daily News* in 1923. During the debate over Glover's appointment, RB referred to the publications in denominational meetings and then summarised his addresses in a pamphlet, *Dr T. R. Glover and the Presidency of the Baptist Union* (1924). RB explained that he did not want to be considered an 'Ishmael' but felt he had to speak out against such an appointment.[1] In his view, a battle was raging 'between two religions', as Gresham Machen had recently expressed, or, as described in *The Christian Century*, between 'Fundamentalism and Modernism'.[2] Spurgeon had drawn attention to dangerous trends in the Baptist Union, but matters had now been accentuated beyond 'even his wildest dreams'.[3] RB quoted Glover at length. He deplored the fact that Glover regarded the Bible just as any other book and that he referred to verbal inspiration as 'a monstrous belief'.[4] Some parts of the Old Testament were 'pagan',[5] Genesis could not be accepted literally,[6] and speaking with tongues should not be attributed to the Holy

157

Spirit.[7] RB believed that Glover was flippant in his style and that he was guilty of misrepresenting the orthodox doctrine, especially the doctrine of atonement, which involved, in Glover's words, the changing of the mind of God.[8] Not only was Glover flippant, but he held 'blasphemous and infidel views'.[9] He could say that 'Jesus is not to be taken quite literally', and that 'Darwin made it necessary to rethink all Christian theology'.[10] Glover had taken the Bible away from Baptists and opened the way to an attack on Christ. He could not find the Jesus of history and had no Christ of experience.

The first significant event in the controversy that ensued took place in Tabernacle, Porth, itself. A Bible Training School student who was a member in the church protested against the appointment of Glover as Vice-president of the Baptist Union.[11] RB and the church decided to pursue the matter and it was raised in the Baptist District Meeting held at Tabernacle.[12] There was not enough time for discussion and it was agreed that it should be introduced at the next District Meeting at Carmel, Pontypridd, on 27 March 1924.

The Resolution, introduced by RB, 'labouring under strong emotion',[13] was as follows:

That the churches of the Pontypridd and Rhondda District of the East Glamorgan Association hereby voice their feeling of perplexity at the election of Dr T. R. Glover to the Vice-Presidency of the Baptist Union, and while sincerely admiring Dr Glover's eminent literary and scholarly attainments, would wish to be assured whether or no the election means that the Baptist Union is to be regarded as having identified itself with Dr Glover's published theological views.[14]

An eyewitness described the scene:

In a quiet, clear tone he commenced his speech. Ere long we became conscious that someone had been tampering with the Wells of Salvation. All the Isaacs there, who hitherto had not had the vision nor the zeal to protest, though the Philistines had filled the wells with stones, were ashamed beyond measure. In the speaker's hand we saw 'Modernism' unmasked. There it lay, a venomous viper, hissing and darting its fangs even at the Son of God. We thought of the undiscerning mass that had cherished it as harmless, and hearts became sick with fear and indignation. For over an hour Mr. Jones spoke. Some faces became dark with fear and hatred, but the majority were set in solemn determination to respond to the call of God through his servant; to stand up in the defence of the truth, and to guard the precious deposit, even with life itself.[15]

The tone of the address was much more aggressive than that of the Resolution.

The next step was to continue the discussion in one of the Baptist Union gatherings at Cardiff. This meeting proceeded more quietly than had been anticipated, however, and RB and his supporters had to be content with the fact that they had made their protest. T. R. Glover himself was present at Cardiff and was given a warm welcome. In the weeks following these Union meetings he was still being eulogised and RB criticised. The most extreme of RB's critics claimed that he had been humiliated.[16] This man was H. H. Williams from Gaerwen, Anglesey. He greatly admired Glover and rebuked RB for claiming monopoly of the truth. He cautioned him that believers in every generation should be ready to follow the leading of the Spirit.[17] His was a purely subjective response. Another correspondent believed that Glover was wholly faithful to Christ and

to his cross, and this, he claimed, was also the opinion of
W. Y. Fullerton, a Keswick man.[18]

The Infallibility of the Man Jesus Christ

Occasionally RB disagreed even with those who were
close to him. Jessie Penn-Lewis sent a series of articles to
him, entitled 'Jesus Christ and Him Crucified'. She
intended to publish them but, before doing so, wanted his
opinion. In his response, RB listed thirty-three points for
her attention. Some of his comments were quite sharp. The
author quoted Dr Mabie quite often, agreeing with his suggestion that the death of Christ was 'entirely new', in that
it was not mortal dying but 'immortal dying', bringing the
sinner into an 'organic union with the risen Christ'. RB
wrote in pencil on his personal copy, 'This is nonsense.' In
his letter to Jessie Penn-Lewis he stated, 'I can only confess that Dr Mabie's terms and phrases thus stressed hinder
me more than they help.'[19] When Jessie Penn-Lewis
referred to 'The complete death–resurrection energy of
Christ mid-process', RB's response was two exclamation
marks and 'Oh!'[20] In a number of places RB pointed out
that Jessie Penn-Lewis had missed the significance of the
tenses of the verbs, especially those in Romans, chapters 6
and 7.[21]

The one book by R. B. Jones that created the most tension between himself and some of his friends was *The
Infallibility of the Man Jesus Christ* (1925). He discussed
the theme in the light of the doctrinal developments of the
day. The inspiration and authority of Scripture had been
attacked, and this had led, as Delitzsch had predicted, to an
attack on the Person of the Lord Jesus Christ.[22] This stray-
ing from the path of orthodoxy began in the theological
colleges and, by the 1920s, 'The whisper of the lecture
room is now the clarion note of the platform.'[23]

RB pinpointed two matters of concern. Firstly, the distinction that was being made between the Jesus of history and the Christ of experience. The critics had been clever enough to discover the Jesus of history 'that long lay hidden beneath the rubbish of Paul's dogma'.[24] The Holy Spirit had been active in the Church over the centuries, but it had been left to the critics to find the real Jesus! And the person whom they claimed was the real Jesus was 'a Shakespeare–cum Charles Lamb–cum Darwin Christ'.[25] The second matter for concern was the Kenotic theory concerning the Person of Christ. RB acknowledged that this teaching had to be taken seriously but did not believe that the 'exegetical battle' had been won.[26]

In spite of serious deviation, the Kenotists had safeguarded the true humanity of the Lord Jesus Christ. RB criticised his fellow evangelicals for neglecting this aspect of the Person of the Saviour. He was a real man: 'So occupied have we been with His Deity that we have almost forgotten this side of his person.'[27]

RB based his argument on two contrasting texts of Scripture: Jesus Christ is the 'Only begotten' (John 1:14), signifying his Deity, and he is the 'First-begotten' (Hebrews 1:6), signifying his humanity.[28] He is the God–man. The Lord Jesus Christ, of himself, could not do or say anything (John 5:30). In becoming man,

> He accepted the limitations, as He did everything else from God. And limitations, of course, there were. Our Lord was man, and man is not infinite. In becoming man God the Son submitted to the limitations and restraints inherent in human existence.[29]

Jesus Christ was a baby, an infant, and grew to manhood. He grew, and had to be made perfect.

In Christ, ignorance and omniscience are wedded together. He did not know the time of his Second Coming (Mark 13:32). RB argued that Christ willed not to know, and was therefore an 'offset' to Adam. Adam's sinful ambition is in contrast to the Lord's willing obedience.[30] His true humanity does not suggest fallibility. Fallen humanity is fallible, but Christ was sinless. Christ spoke with authority and was infallible. His finitude never degenerated to fallibility, because his dependence on God was complete. It is strange that RB does not bring in the ministry of the Holy Spirit in this context, because it was the Spirit that safeguarded this relationship between the humanity and deity of Christ.

It would be better, according to RB, to speak of 'plerosis' rather than 'kenosis'.[31] The truly human Christ received everything from God, and whatever comes from God is authoritative:

> To hear Him is to hear God. He is the Truth. No shame can ever come to those who place their implicit trust in His every word.[32]

In general RB argued clearly and strongly, although occasionally he could indulge in sarcastic comments. At times, perhaps, he was too bold in his statements, but there is no doubt that he was right in insisting on the true humanity of the Lord Jesus Christ. Some of RB's friends, however, were perturbed. They wrote to him to discuss many points in his work.

The main bone of contention was the reference to the 'limitations' of Christ. J. P. Wiles took exception to RB's claim that the orthodox had almost forgotten Christ's humanity. Wiles regarded this a reproach 'against *yourself & me & all our godly* friends'.[33] He had been upset by the reference to 'limitations':

Incarnate God knew nothing of limitations. This new line of thought has nothing in the Bible to give it even apparent support . . . Scripture never speaks of Christ's limitations, the phrase seems to me to have been made in Germany.[34]

Responding to RB's statement of the mystery of 'ignorance wedded with omniscience', Wiles declared, 'I strongly protest against its very use by anybody.'[35] Wiles did not believe that Mark 13:32 was a confession of ignorance, but he gave no clear reasons for his claim.

In replying to Wiles, RB acknowledged that at some points he could have expressed himself more clearly. For example, instead of referring to 'human life' at one point, he should have said 'man in personal union'. But he would not change his mind regarding his central argument. He buttressed his case by quoting from Torrey's *What the Bible Teaches*, a work that was studied in the Bible Training Institute. RB summarised Torrey's points on 'limitation': (1) Physical considerations. (2) Limitation of knowledge. (3) Christ's temptation. (4) Christ prayed. (5) He needed the Holy Spirit. (6) He was limited in the exercise of his power.[36] These were helpful points, though this last point needed fuller explanation. Why should Christ's humanity necessarily limit his exercise of power?

A further correspondent, Sydney Collett, argued that Mark 13:32 was wrongly translated in the AV and referred to his own work, *Scriptures of Truth*; but he did not include his translation in his letter. In any case, he argued, Mark 13:32 is only one verse, and there is overwhelming evidence that Christ knew everything.[37] Another correspondent, H. D. Woolley, quoted Isaiah 50:4 (RV) in order to explain Mark 13:32. He had also asked R. B. Girdlestone's opinion on the word 'emptied' in Philippians 2:7, and although he believed that 'emptied' could be justified grammatically, he thought that the AV rendering was the more correct in the particular context of the verse. Woolley therefore believed that the AV version safeguarded the omniscience of Christ.[38]

It is difficult to understand how Wiles and the others would not consider any degree of 'limitation' at all. Their attitude was really proving RB's point with respect to the neglect of the true humanity of Christ. On the other hand, RB was exaggerating the nature of that neglect, in that men like Irenaeus, Athanasius, Anselm, Luther and John Owen had contributed considerably to the development of this doctrine.

There is no doubt that feelings were hurt. RB makes this clear when replying to J. P. Wiles:

> You will not be surprised when I say that your words pain me beyond expression, while at the same time I know your conviction and your love.[39]

The controversy shows that RB could map out his own path, however much it hurt him to disagree with friends. It is only fair to add that to enter into controversy with those who disagreed with him was not always easy for him.

Spiritism in Bible Light
RB, however, was always ready to act as a defender of the faith. He made use of *Yr Efengylydd* to this end, as, for example, when criticising the teaching of Frank Buchman on Moral Re-armament.[40] And he also contributed a detailed work on Spiritism (*Spiritism in Bible Light*, 1920), a series of lectures first delivered at his weekly Bible School.

In introducing this subject, RB claimed: 'We are met to consider what is rapidly becoming one of the greatest characteristics of our day—the spread of what is known as Spiritism.'[41]

This should be no surprise to those who acknowledge the existence of the presence of 'the dark figure who inspires all such movements'. Basic to an understanding of Spiritism and similar movements is the acceptance of the personal reality of the Devil. RB deals with the terms 'Devil', 'Satan', 'Lucifer', 'dragon', and 'prince of this world'.[42] In his kingdom—that of 'this world'—Satan works directly and indirectly through the instrumentality of humans and evil spirits. The author quotes Ezekiel 28:11-19 as a scripture that gives an understanding of the origin and work of Satan, and relates the passage to Isaiah 14:12-14 and Revelation 20:10. He then elaborates further on 'Satan's System'.[43]

The second chapter of the book is devoted to the history of Spiritism. RB provides a word study of such Old Testament words as 'spirits', 'magician', and 'soothsayer',[44] and New Testament words discussed are 'sorcery' and 'idolatry'.[45]

In dealing with the account of the Witch of Endor, RB comes to the conclusion that 'the spirit of the dead prophet really appeared'. It did not appear, however, at the command of the witch: 'Samuel was here by God's permission, and the bearer of an awful message of doom to the fallen king'.[46] RB confirms his argument in three ways: firstly, by referring to Samuel's 'disinclination to appear', unlike a spirit in a séance; secondly, by the import of the condemnation expressed—'the Lord is departed from thee, and is become thine enemy'; and lastly, by quoting 1 Chronicles 10:13-14, where the 'crowning crime' was 'asking counsel of one who had a familiar spirit'.[47]

165

The spread of Spiritism is traced in chapter 3 from the work of the Fox family in America to Conan Doyle and Oliver Lodge. The movement was given an impetus by the growth in Psychical Research and the harrowing experiences of the First World War. Spiritists believed that different manifestations were proofs of survival after death. RB mentions some of these in chapter 4: 'materialisation', 'levitation' and 'clairvoyance'.[48] In his response, RB makes the point that some of these cases could be explained on natural grounds. Scientific research had developed, giving a clearer understanding of the subconscious. In particular situations, powers that are latent in the sub-conscious may be exercised in a trance, for example, or in a dream. Telepathy might account for some cases, because mind may directly influence mind without the instrumentality of words.[49] There is, however, no need for seeking other supernatural opinions, in that the Scriptures present a message of living hope in Christ, and proclaim that all believers who have died are with Christ.

In chapter 5, RB discusses in more detail the Bible's condemnation of Spiritism, and then in chapter 6 proceeds to expose the dangers of Spiritism—physical, mental and moral. Chapter 7 is devoted to showing the doctrinal weaknesses of Spiritism in its teaching with regard to God, the Scriptures, the Lord Jesus Christ, and the atonement. The whole system fails because it has a wrong view of God. He is portrayed as impersonal. What is based on that premise cannot be right. RB had no doubt at all that Spiritism is anti-Christian.

It is typical of R. B. Jones's doctrinal emphases, as already discussed, that the title of the last chapter is 'Dispensational Significance'. Spiritism, he argues, is part of the falling away before the Second Coming of Christ.

Spiritism is by far the most menacing of all present-day
dangers, and, from the point of view of Bible prophecy,
by far the most significant of the signs of our times.[50]

The Bible outlines the whole course of history, and does so
by denoting seven dispensations. The end of the sixth
period—that of grace—is described as 'the latter days'.
Those days are of real significance in Scripture:

Indeed, one cannot be far wrong in saying that it is
mainly in connection with that end-time that Bible pre-
diction at all descends to particulars in its description of
the future.[51]

It will be a time of lawlessness, anarchy and supernatural-
ism (2 Timothy 3:1; 2 Thessalonians 2:7-10).[52]

One author had suggested that the Man of Sin would be
the offspring of 'a materialised demon and a woman who
will sell herself to him for that degrading purpose'.[53] RB
believed that there was much to support this view:

This at least is certain, that all these false teachings,
Spiritist teachings especially, are following a line of
development which must find its climax in that vile
blasphemer who will oppose himself to all that is God.
We are to-day in the midst of movements, inspired by
Satan, such, perhaps, as this earth has not witnessed
this side of the Deluge.[54]

Already, in his own day, RB believed that the earth was
'becoming overwhelmed by a host of demons who know
that their doom cannot be much longer delayed'.[55] The
author closes the book with a warning and an exhortation:

If ever lamps should be burning, and loins girded, they
should be today.[56]

There was great need for such a work as *Spiritism in Bible Light*, and RB deals thoroughly with his subject. He was on firm ground when discussing different biblical aspects, and revealed a sound knowledge of the nature and history of Spiritism. He displays, however, a tendency to be obsessed with the idea of demons and to be at times too sarcastic. His interpretation of the 'latter days' is also unsatisfactory. He does not provide evidence for his views, and a greater emphasis on Christ's victory over all powers and principalities would have strengthened the work.

10
Hymns and hymn tunes

ONE thing that marked R. B. Jones was his love of
music. He had learned to play the piano when young
and enjoyed the excellent congregational singing at his
home church, Hebron, Dowlais. He had a good singing
voice and could make use of it in presenting the gospel, as
he did during the visit of James Oatey to Ainon, Ynys-hir.[1]
During the 1904–5 Revival, he was always happy to have
the support of soloists—David Ellis would sing in his services, as would the two brothers, Arthur and Emlyn Davies.[2]
He also enjoyed listening to classical music.[3] Before his
visit to America in 1907, he produced a collection of
hymns and hymn tunes.

Prayer and Praise
The full title of the collection was *Prayer and
Praise/Gweddi a Mawl. A Collection of English and Welsh
Hymns for Use in Mission Services Conducted by R. B.
Jones, Porth (Wales).*[4] These services were held in America
from February to May 1907, and were arranged by the
Welsh Baptist churches of Northern Pennsylvania. The
collection included 109 Welsh and 50 English hymns. The
sources of some of the hymn tunes were noted on the first
page: *Hymns of Consecration and Faith, Alexander's New
Revival Hymnal,* and *Christian Choir.* RB added others in
his own handwriting: *Llawlyfr Moliant, Pentecostal Hymns,
Sacred Songs and Solos, Heavenly Sunlight, Baptist
Hymnal, Temple Chimes, Church Hymns, Gospel Songs,*

169

Sunday School Hymns, Choice Hymns, and *Songs of the Century.*

The choice of tunes and words reveal RB's catholic taste and his breadth of interest and knowledge. Hymns from different denominational hymnals, and hymns both old and new, are included. The authors are not identified, but there are familiar hymns by Isaac Watts, Frances Ridley Havergal, William Williams (Pantycelyn), John Roberts (*Ieuan Gwyllt*), Charles Wesley and Charlotte Elliott.

In both English and Welsh sections the influence of the Revival is evident. Favourites of the Revival are included: hymns such as 'There is a fountain filled with blood' (No. 4), 'When all my labours and trials are o'er' (No. 33) and 'All hail the power of Jesus' name' (No. 48). In the Welsh section we find: *'Ai Iesu, Cyfaill dynolryw'* (No. 40); *'A welsoch chwi Ef?'* (No. 60); *'Gwaed y Groes sy'n codi i fyny'* (No. 66), and *'Felly carodd Duw wrthrychau'* (No. 95).

'A welsoch chwi Ef?' is a translation from English, and other translations from English are, *'Duw mawr y rhyfeddodau maith'* (No. 26), *'Pan ar fordaith bywyd'* (No. 34), and *'Pan ddelo terfyn ar lafur a loes'* (No. 57).

RB also chose English translations of Welsh hymns that had been sung with feeling in the Revival: 'Here is love, unfathomed, shoreless' (No. 26); 'Ride in triumph' (No. 6); 'At Calvary's Cross I cast away' (No. 20); 'In Eden, I remember well' (No. 21); 'Say, have you seen Him?' (No. 22); 'Calvary's blood the faint one raises' (No. 29), and 'Recall the righteous Jesus' (No. 32).

Some of the hymns continue the Revival practice of adding lines to the original hymns. Thus, RB added two lines to the hymn, 'When I survey the wondrous Cross' (No. 7):

When I survey the wondrous Cross
On which the Prince of glory died,
To set the captive free;
My richest gain I count but loss,
And pour contempt on all my pride;
O! wondrous Calvary.

Often, the following verse was added to a hymn:

Oh! The Lamb, the bleeding Lamb,
The Lamb of Calvary;
The Lamb that was slain—He liveth again,
To intercede for me.

RB added it to the translation of Pantycelyn's hymn, 'At Calvary's Cross I cast away' (No. 20).

The editor included a number of his own hymns. Twelve hymns can be identified as RB's work—six of them are translations, and six are original. The originals of the six translations are found in *Hymns of Consecration and Faith*. Three of them have survived: '*Tra y byddwn yn byw*'—'When we walk with the Lord' (No. 88, Welsh section; No. 1, English section); '*Moliant i Ti, fwyn Waredwr*' —'How I praise Thee' (No. 79 and No. 19), and '*O! dwg fi'n nes i'th fynwes Iesu*'—'Let me come closer to Thee, Jesus' (No. 78 and No. 36). The first of these was included in *Molwch Dduw* (Apostolic Church, Pen-y-groes, 1954), and all three of them in *Telyn Seion* (London, n.d.), a selection of hymns used in the Ammanford Whitsun Convention.

It is difficult to find one of RB's translations that is completely satisfactory. He succeeds with individual verses, but not with a hymn as a whole. The translation of 'When we walk with the Lord' is well done, but occasionally he adds to the meaning or does not fully bring out the original. His translation of 'Until all on the altar we lay', for example, as '*Hyd nes plygwn yn isel i'r iau*' refers to a 'yoke' rather than an 'altar'. However, he does succeed with the last verse:

> *Mewn cymundeb difrad,*
> *Eistedd wnawn wrth Ei draed;*
> *Yn Ei gwmni y mynnwn barhau;*
> *'R hyn a ddywed a wnawn,*
> *Lle y mynno yr awn,*
> *Gan ymddiried a llwyr ufuddhau.*

A characteristic of his original Welsh hymns is the scriptural references provided above each one of them, and the hymns clearly reflect the themes of those verses. Above one hymn, for example (No. 88), are references to Romans 6:1-11; 7:1-4, and Galatians 2:19 and 6:14. The hymn-writer expresses amazement that he is dead and yet alive. He was crucified with Christ in order to live for Christ. Consequently, he died to the law, to sin, to the world, and to self. The life lived in the flesh is lived by faith in the Son of God.

This theme of new life in Christ is, in fact, a recurring thread in all RB's hymns. The believer is crucified with Christ, and Christ lives in the believer. How wondrous was the sight of Christ as a baby in a manger, but it is more wondrous still that he can live in the heart of a sinner! The Christian life is one of holiness, but it will be not realised without a specific commitment to Christ. It is an act of commitment, of trusting in God's promises and not depending on feelings. Twice in his hymns, RB uses the phrase 'to receive sanctification'; his Keswick doctrine of sanctification is very evident in them. In some of his hymns there is a lack of feeling, and at times the author fails to express his theme clearly and his lines become cumbersome.

Not only did R. B. Jones contribute hymns, but he also composed hymn tunes. One of his daughters recalls how her father would

> often compose hymn tunes in bed. After his Sunday afternoon preparation in his locked bedroom, he would come down and play records of oratorios, negro spirituals and classical music.[5]

He gave careful attention to the music of the collection. In one version of the work he included a choice of tunes, identifying them both by name and by their number in published hymn-books. Although he refers to a number of sources, it is clear that he had a preference for *Llawlyfr Moliant* (The Welsh Baptist Hymn Book, 1899). In both Welsh and English sections, for every hymn the first line of the music is given in sol-fa.

When RB composed hymn tunes he would name them after family members or places dear to him. Familiar names are 'Lizzie'—his first wife, 'Menna'—one of his daughters and 'Derlwyn'—his home. He wrote tunes for words that appealed to him. 'Menna' is a tune set to the hymn 'I heard the voice of Jesus say', and 'Derlwyn' to 'Just as I am, without one plea'.

One example of an English hymn by RB[6]
It is possible that RB is the author of some of the English hymns in *Prayer and Praise*. There is no doubt, however, about his authorship of another hymn that is not found in that collection—'Thou hast won my heart to love Thee'. This hymn is signed R. B. J. and bears the Scripture reference Mark 12:30:[7]

Mark 12:30   *R. B. J.*

Thou hast won my *heart* to love Thee,
  Blessèd Jesus, Son Divine;
From the world and all its idols
  Thou hast weaned me, I am Thine:
Henceforth on Thy bosom leaning,
  Just like John, I fain would be,
For I love Thee, Blessèd Jesus,
  Since Thou first hast lovèd me.

Thou hast won my *soul* to love Thee,
  Blessèd Jesus, Friend Divine;
All its faculties, emotions,
  Its affections—all are thine:
All its strings, made holy, yielding
  To Thy touch sweet melody;
For I love Thee, Blessèd Jesus,
  Since Thou first hast lovèd me.

Thou hast won my *mind* to love Thee,
  Blessèd Jesus, Truth Divine;
Into all my nature's darkness
  Thou hast made Thy glory shine:
Ever gazing on Thy beauty,
  By that vision changed I'd be;
For I love Thee, Blessèd Jesus,
  Since Thou first hast lovèd me.

Thou hast won my *strength* to love Thee,
  Blessèd Jesus, King Divine;
Blood-redeemed, my body's yielded;
  All its powers now are Thine:

So with busy hands and footsteps
  I would e'er Thy servant be;
For I love Thee, Blessèd Jesus,
  Since thou first hast lovèd me.

Chorus
  Yes, I love Thee, Blessèd Saviour,
    I have nought but love for Thee;
  Yet I long to love Thee ever
    With that love Thou hast for me.

11
Last days and evaluation

At the beginning of 1933 RB was very tired, and Dr Martyn Lloyd-Jones, Aberafan, advised him to rest, suggesting that a sea cruise might help him recover.[1] RB managed to preach on the first Sunday of April, and on the following Monday kept an engagement in Dover. A few days later, he left with his son Geraint on a Mediterranean cruise, but having arrived at Port Said, Egypt, he collapsed and had to come home. He was confined to bed and watched over by his devoted wife Catherine, but he died on 15 April. Messages of condolence poured in and a number of newspapers carried an obituary.[2]

On 20 April 1933, the ladies of Tabernacle and Bethlehem, Porth, prepared two meals for those coming to attend the funeral of their respected pastor.

> The buses began to come in at 11 o'clock, from Anglesey, Caernarvon and Wrexham, Llanelly, Swansea and Carmarthen. From 10 o'clock until 1, there had been about 4 to 500 people feeding in the vestry.[3]

Tabernacle was full for the funeral service, with people standing three abreast in the aisles and crowds waiting outside. Two unusual circumstances in the service were the placing of a Bible, open at Romans 6, on the coffin, and the leading of the singing of 'Crown him Lord of all' by his wife Mrs Catherine Jones. Mourners included the family, a large number of ministers, prominent men such as Evan

Roberts and an ex-president of the Baptist Union, present and former students of the Bible Institute, church members, and many others not belonging to any church. Shops on the funeral route were closed, and crowds gathered on the streets between Hannah Street and the cemetery at Trealaw.[4] Porth had never before witnessed such a scene. The funeral was a tribute to a man of God.

R. B. Jones's personality

Physically, RB was good-looking, and of a sturdy frame. There was in him a mixture of firmness and pleasantness. He could be severe and aggressive and yet, in another context, humble and kind. When the truths he cherished so much were attacked, 'He would fall upon the luckless Agag and hew him to pieces.' On the other hand, he was a man who could faint after having had to carry one of his children to an ambulance to be taken to hospital.[5] Some people thought him unapproachable, while others valued his friendship. He was a man much hated and much loved. J. R. Morgan summarises his character:

> One cannot think of R. B. Jones without remembering the dignity of his being. In the pulpit, in the street, and in the house. It was characteristic of him. It attracted notice and no doubt commanded respect and attention to the message heralded forth. This was a distinct feature of his personality, and perhaps to those not very intimate with him suggested possibly that he was reserved and unapproachable. No doubt it did keep many aloof who might otherwise have found in him a very sincere and pure human heart.[6]

People in the streets would either acknowledge him with reverence or avoid him. When a difficult decision had to be taken, R. B. Jones could be bold. A former student relates one example of a characteristic action. RB believed that carnivals were worldly and a waste of time. On one occasion, knowing that the carnival was due down his street, he walked to meet it, held up his hand and stopped it from proceeding further.[7] On the other hand, when he felt that circumstances required it, he could accept a compromise. The father of one of the students was a cripple and enjoyed smoking. RB, though firmly against smoking, could sympathise with him: 'Crippled as you are, I am certain that the good Lord doesn't grudge you that bit of pleasure.'[8]

The minister of Tabernacle was serious, especially so in the pulpit, but he also had a sense of humour. A minister complained to RB of the divisions in one particular church. A new cause had been formed, and soon there was a further division in the new church. Again, one man had separated himself from one of the parties and was breaking bread on his own. RB responded, 'Poor fellow! The Lord help him if he has a split. He will need a post-mortem!'[9] And there were two ministers that could make RB laugh. These were Baptist ministers Morgan Jones (Whitland) and Jubilee Young (Llanelli). Whenever Jubilee Young imitated John Thomas, another Baptist minister, RB could not refrain from laughing. (Jubilee Young could also do an excellent imitation of RB himself.)[10]

RB's general attitude towards those with whom he disagreed is often not appreciated or remembered. Though critical of socialism, he was very friendly in his approach to a man like Arthur J. Cook, Marxist General Secretary of the Miners' Federation of Great Britain. When Cook was taking meetings in the area, he would attend Tabernacle to hear RB, and according to his son Geraint, 'One of the last letters that A. J. Cook received on his death bed was one from my father of sympathy and encouragement.'[11]

Herbert Morgan, an advocate of the social gospel, was brought up under RB's ministry. It was RB who gathered sufficient financial support for his studies at Mansfield College, Oxford. In response, probably, to this kindness, Herbert Morgan invited RB to preach in Castle Street, London. RB was glad to accept, but when he preached on 'You must be born again', the atmosphere changed considerably. When it came to preaching, the truth was at stake.

Lloyd George, Chancellor of the Exchequer at the time, and William Jones, Member of Parliament for Arfon, were in the congregation. Knowing that there would be tension, William Jones stood up to speak at the end of the service in order to keep the peace. Lloyd George then invited an 'angry Herbert Morgan', D. R. Daniel (a Welsh political publicist), William Jones and RB to supper at 11 Downing Street. Here again William Jones was wise. Instead of referring to the sermon, he brought Abraham Lincoln's name into the conversation, knowing he was one of Lloyd George's heroes, and in the subsequent discussion Herbert Morgan and RB had no opportunity to bring up the new birth.[12]

RB possessed a good knowledge of current affairs but would not become involved in the social issues of his day. On a personal level, however, he was very sensitive to the material as well as the spiritual needs of the people. It grieved him that so many churches in Wales were taken up with *eisteddfodau* and concerts; yet he himself was a cultured man, well-read, able to appreciate music and compose hymns and hymn tunes.

Although labelled a fundamentalist, RB was an enlightened fundamentalist. He was criticised for accepting everything in the Bible literally, and for believing, because of his literalism, that everything in the Bible was of equal value. But very often the critics ignored RB's

actual statements and arguments. One correspondent
claimed that RB and other fundamentalists believed not
only that the original writers of the books of the Bible were
inspired, but that the later copyists and translators were
inspired too. Another correspondent suggested that RB
believed that the authors of Scripture were passive instruments driven by some external power; that the writers
placed themselves in the path of the Spirit, and God spoke
through them.[13]

RB however was quite clear in his doctrine of inspiration:

> The Bible as we have it, in its various translations and
> revisions, when freed from all the errors and mistakes
> of translations, copyists and printers, is the very Word
> of God, and consequently without error.[14]

He refuted the theories of 'intuition', 'illumination' and
'dictation', and argued for 'dynamic inspiration'. Com-
menting on the 'dictation' theory, he stated that it

> could not account for the peculiar style of each human
> writer. Also, much of what they wrote needed not to be
> dictated for they knew it already.

He then gave his own definition:

> Dynamic inspiration denotes the action of the Holy
> Spirit upon living men, working according to the natural
> laws of their minds, and using them as active and not
> passive instruments.[15]

R. B. Jones as a preacher
Above everything else, RB was a preacher. The pulpit was
his castle. He wielded tremendous influence in the United

Kingdom and in many pulpits overseas. He was as effective in English as in Welsh, his mother tongue. From his very first ministry at Berth-lwyd, Treharris, it was evident that he would be a popular preacher. His preparation was thorough; he wrote his sermons in full, and presented his message with conviction.

After the Llandrindod Convention of 1903, a marked change took place in his life and preaching. His friend W. S. Jones described the change. The following is a summary of his words:

1. Compared to his earlier preaching, his texts invariably lent themselves by their exposition to the presentation of the very heart of the Gospel. Formerly, 'The axe did swim' could do for a text, and many good thoughts beautifully expressed would be given. But now it would be, 'I am not ashamed of the Gospel of Christ'.

2. In the treatment of any text, it was his habit, while keeping an eye on the true exposition of the text as a whole, to fix on one thought that would become the burden of his heart and of his sermon. The sermon would then be topical and would become, in his handling of it, a real message. The impression created, almost invariably, was that he had one thing to say in each discourse. And he hammered at it, till everybody understood its importance.

3. As he grew older, the importance of exposition impressed itself upon him, and much more of the sermon than was formerly the case would be given to exposition. Yet the habit of bringing all to bear on one message, and for that one message to be driven home, remained to the end.

4. The expository characteristic of his preaching would not be confined to the local interpretation of his text,

but very, very frequently the point extracted from the text and its connection would be subjected to the light thrown upon it by the teaching of the Bible generally. His knowledge of the Bible as a whole, together with his retentive memory of verses and of their location, was a tremendous asset to him in this respect.

5. It was not an unimportant result of the great spiritual change that he experienced, though it may appear to some of quite secondary import, that he was set free from the shackles of a manuscript. No more was he tied to the words that he had written. It was not that he did not prepare, but that his preparation did not shackle him.[16]

In his sixth and last point, W. S. Jones declared that RB could refer, like Paul, to 'my Gospel', because 'It was God's Gospel, and it was RB's. God had written it on the preacher's heart.'

In his fourth point W. S. Jones mentioned RB's knowledge of the Scriptures. Geraint Jones, one of RB's sons, bears witness to this same characteristic. He used the Bible continually, in the pulpit and at the Institute. He had no trouble at all in turning to any section of the Scriptures:

His own knowledge of the Bible was extraordinary. He knew most of the epistles by heart, and was able to quote freely at length from memory from any part of the Old and New Testaments.[17]

The main themes of RB's preaching were the Cross, Sanctification, Assurance, and the Second Coming of the Lord Jesus Christ. He did Wales a great service by making the atoning death of Christ central to his preaching. This was a doctrine that was under great attack in his day. He contributed significantly also by re-emphasising the doctrine of the Second Coming—a truth that was not only being attacked but ridiculed. It is unfortunate, however, that he spent so much time on the finer details of the Second Coming.

In a day and time when the immanence of God was being emphasised, RB proclaimed the God who is Creator beyond his creation, and yet who came into the world in the Person of the Lord Jesus Christ. It was his work on the Cross that enabled fallen creatures to be restored to fellowship with a holy God.

Evan Roberts had once advised RB not to preach the righteousness of Christ but his love, which he believed was the sweet note of the Revival. RB could not agree. The righteousness and the love of Christ had to be considered together. They should never be separated. This had to be the case because of the nature of God's holiness. It is both righteous and loving, as revealed in the death of the Lord Jesus Christ for sinful men and women.[18] RB was critical of the over-emotionalism that characterised some of Evan Roberts's meetings, and critical also of the revivalist's lack of emphasis on preaching. He was too mystical and too experience-centred. The content of RB's preaching was doctrinal, but he presented his message without any over-use of theological terms.[19]

J. T. Jones (Rhos) commented on RB's preaching:

He made holiness REAL, and he made holiness TERRIBLE. How shall I describe it all? There is no other word for it—it was consuming.[20]

Because of this strong emphasis on God's holiness, RB could appear stern and harsh in the presentation of his message. He was sometimes accused of keeping his congregation too long at the foot of Sinai. There is some truth in such an assessment, but RB was correct in his conviction that congregations had to be brought to Sinai. He was not content, however, to leave them there. Sinners are not converted by loitering at the foot of Sinai but by running to the foot of Calvary, and a great number were converted under the Calvary-ministry of RB.

Aligned with his emphasis on holiness was his tendency to condemn all kinds of activities he regarded as sinful (such as reading novels, going to the cinema or secular concerts). It is appropriate to condemn particular sins, just as the great preacher John Elias used to do, but there are two dangers to be avoided—the danger of being only negative, and the danger of labelling as sinful something that is morally neutral. During the late 1920s, RB became very censorious and severe with respect to moral issues, but he mellowed towards the end of his ministry.

Ithel Jones, RB's nephew, said that the one word to describe RB's preaching was 'passion'.[21] He was not an orator—not a traditional Welsh preacher—and he did not have the '*hwyl*' of some preachers. Reference has already been made to the passionate nature of his preaching in 1904 in Rhosllannerchrugog, but the same characteristic was found right to the end of his ministry in 1933.

It was during a later period that Ithel Jones heard his uncle preaching. He was present at Moriah, Dowlais, when RB's text was, 'But what things were gain to me, those I counted loss for Christ.' Friends of early days were in the gallery, many of them unconverted. After describing graphically Paul's reasons for boasting in the flesh, RB took out a pencil and, drawing an imaginary line through the list, with a fervent shout cried, 'Flesh!' Turning to his old friends in the gallery, he reminded them of his own background that they knew so well, and in a quieter but more passionate voice cried out, 'If anyone can boast, I can.' And suddenly, even more fervently than the first shout, came the cry, 'Dung and loss!' The congregation was spellbound.[22]

It could be argued that RB was one of the great preachers of Wales. It could also be argued that he was one of the most travelled of Welsh preachers. Howell Harris travelled extensively, but he never had to maintain a settled ministry at the same time. RB had such a ministry, but he also travelled throughout Britain and overseas. It is doubtful if, since the eighteenth century, there was a more sustained and fruitful ministry. The manifestation of the Holy Spirit was evident throughout his ministry. He taught and evangelised regularly. During his ministry at Porth, six members departed to work overseas and ten others to work with home missions. It is worth noting, however, that Keri Evans experienced an unction of the Spirit every day for twenty years; yet in his ministry the visible fruit was not so marked. His was a different kind of service; he was primarily a teacher. RB was preacher, teacher and evangelist combined.

Wherever R. B. Jones preached, people flocked to hear him. He never tried to be a popular preacher. There were no histrionics in the pulpit, no vivid illustrations and no sentimental stories. He did not desire popularity, but scores of people idolised him. Tabernacle was full every Sunday, and an appreciable number from all parts of the Rhondda and beyond would attend his week-night services.

Some of the tributes paid to RB as a preacher are quite remarkable. The views of Ithel Jones and J. T. Jones have already been given. Two other opinions, from very different sources, may be added. The *News Chronicle* believed that

No one was better known, and it is a certainty that since the days of the Great Revival no one has exercised a

185

greater influence over the masses than this uncompromising exponent of the Gospel. Wherever he went a great multitude was eager to listen, and with a small band of kindred souls he has kept the evangelical fire alive in his native land. He preached with the zeal and dead-sureness of John Wesley, and in eloquence few have excelled him since the days of John Elias.[23]

His son Geraint Jones states:

For myself, I have never heard any one able to preach on a Biblical theme with more breadth of vision and majesty, nor have I ever seen very large congregations sit in such a fixed and still attention from the moment the towering pulpit personality came to his feet to begin in quiet, simple language until the end of the memorable, unfolding theme was reached an hour or more later.[24]

When, in 1919, Dr Arthur C. Dixon retired from the pastorate of the Metropolitan Tabernacle, London, Dr McCaig asked the Rev. Caradoc Jones if there was anyone in Wales who might be considered as his successor, and the reply was 'R. B. Jones'. RB in fact accepted an invitation to preach and was given a Sunday at the Metropolitan Tabernacle, but in the meantime a call was extended to, and accepted by, Dr H. Tydeman Chilvers.[25] Caradoc Jones could think of only one appropriate name from Wales, and that man would have been a worthy successor to Spurgeon.

In his day he was commended for preaching to the conscience. O. M. Owen, a friend of RB's, could say of him:

He preached to the conscience throughout his life. I wonder if Wales has heard anyone compared with him in this respect, since the death of Owen Thomas, Liverpool.[26]

And, like Owen Thomas, RB was also 'a preacher of the people'. He, in turn, influenced his students, and sent them out to preach the same gospel in the same simple way.

RB was given the opportunity to exercise both his preaching and his teaching gifts through the medium of the Bible Training School/Bible Institute. He was the founder, the Principal, and the main organiser of every aspect of the life of the School. His was an honorary Principalship, in that he refused payment for his work at the Institute. He also insisted on paying the £125–£130 p.a. that covered the full-board and residence costs for himself and his family.[27] This was typical behaviour.

> His generosity was astonishing. I have come to the conclusion that he gave away about half of his income from all sources, to causes he supported and the considerable number of individuals he was moved to help and he died a poor man.[28]

He was always giving.

The Institute was based on a clearly defined doctrinal basis and on rigid rules. One result of such an arrangement was the isolation of the School, not only from other theological colleges, but also from society generally. He thought this was essential if he was to realise his vision of a thoroughly biblically-based school. Too great an emphasis on his narrowness and rigidity would, however, be inaccurate, for the students highly regarded their Principal; indeed they loved him. The school was a family, and RB its father. To the students he was a great preacher and an effective lecturer, but he was great and effective primarily because of his character. He practised what he preached, and he not only urged them to be godly but demonstrated godliness in his own life.

Keri Evans pinpointed 'spiritual atmosphere' as the characteristic of the life of the School, adding, 'In this connection Religious Wales will, I believe, be under a lasting debt to RB.' The debt was twofold:

1. For bringing back the Faith of God to its appropriate position even in the machinery of the Theological College and the Church.

2. For placing the chief emphasis on a spiritual training in the education given by a theological college.[29]

The outworking of such principles was seen in the emphasis on conversion, holiness, prayer, and other practical aspects, as well in the nature of the teaching provided.

R. B. Jones as college principal

The original name, 'The Bible Training School for Christian Workers', expressed the real aim that RB had in mind: that is, the training of committed men and women for every possible aspect of Christian service. There is no doubt that the practical instruction was better at Porth than it was in other colleges in Wales. Women were included among the students and departed to work in churches, missions and homes. At least one woman was set apart to preach, though RB did not provide any scriptural justification for this act. A remarkably high number of students went to work overseas, and overseas students came to Porth and then returned to their own country. This was one of the most valuable contributions of the School/Institute. For Porth Institute and for RB, the world was the parish.

It was a Baptist Institute. It is true that in theory it was open to all evangelicals irrespective of denominational allegiance, but in practice believers' baptism by immersion was the only baptism that was acceptable. As a convinced Baptist, RB may not be blamed for safeguarding Baptist principles, but it is unfortunate that he did not make a greater effort to include others of different persuasions within the College set-up. He himself could see the doctrinal decline in other denominational schools, and he could have developed a college with an appeal that extended over a much wider front.

In the light of the full extent of RB's contribution, it is difficult to accept all the strictures that Iain H. Murray raises in his critique of RB and his work in his two-volume biography of Martyn Lloyd-Jones.[30] He is quite in order in mentioning that RB was impressionable, that he could be censorious, and that he was too much taken up with holiness and prophetic movements. Some of his statements, however, must be challenged.

Murray shows a lack of respect for RB's theological understanding. He states that RB 'failed to discern' the difference between the old Methodist preaching and the new preaching introduced to Wales through Charles Finney, and that RB, like others in Wales, 'lacked real theological understanding'. RB was no Calvinist, but the content and method of his preaching were certainly not in the tradition of Finney. To say so would be to ignore the testimony of bundles of sermons in the National Library in Aberystwyth, and the testimony of those who heard RB preach. His sermons were clear on the new birth, the deity of Christ, the atoning death of Christ, and on heaven and hell. RB could appeal for people to come forward in a meeting, but he could also send a congregation to their homes so that each one might spend time alone with his God. RB's Arminianism was not that of Charles Finney.

Bound up with these claims are two other statements. Iain Murray refers to the 'amalgam' of RB's teaching, 'reflected in the absence of any clearly recognisable theological position in the teachings of his Bible Institute at Porth'.[31] On the contrary, the Porth Institute had a clear doctrinal statement.

The other statement is this:

> Frequently his preaching was denunciatory and Porth, instead of being a centre for a growing number of Christians, became a *cul de sac* for adherents to a declining cause—a cause which, to some extent, merited the negative and anti-intellectual image which it came to possess in South Wales.[32]

It is true that RB was much criticised for his denunciatory preaching, but there is no proof at all that this was responsible for a decrease in the number of students attending at Porth. Indeed, the evidence is to the contrary. In 1929, the number of students in the Institute was forty-two, twenty of them being new students. The congregations at Tabernacle were still strong, and the inhabitants of Rhondda and of other places further afield still flocked to the weekly and monthly meetings at Porth. There was no sign of decline.

Furthermore, former students and supporters of RB would be appalled to read that Porth was a *cul de sac*. Such a judgement is harsh and unjust. Porth was no *cul de sac*; it was rather a highway for service. About forty of its students went overseas, together with the fourteen or so foreign students that went back to work in their own countries. The church at Tabernacle was also missionary-minded. Former students of the Institute were scattered over Wales and amongst city missions such as Liverpool and London. There was a decline of numbers in the Institute after RB's death, but the reasons for this were a combination of doctrinal and personal matters that eventually led to a division in 1936.

There is some truth in Iain Murray's charge of 'anti-intellectualism'. RB was at fault in this matter. In his lecture room he could deal substantially with some difficult problems. In his theology course, for example, he devoted five lectures to 'Kenosis', and he lectured on the unity of Isaiah, arguing that the external evidence for dividing the book was 'scant', as acknowledged by Skinner, and raising further considerations such as the nature of prophecy and the witness of the New Testament.[33] He had both the ability and the knowledge to discuss such matters. He once suggested to a fellow minister that he should read Karl Barth.[34] On the other hand, RB would frequently dismiss the attack of the modernists out of hand, often by ridiculing them. He could say, for example,

> Were it not for the seriousness of the matter, one would be tempted to laugh at what is largely a display of silly childishness.[35]

It was not the best way to deal with the growth and challenge of Modernism.

Another point that must be mentioned is that of denominational allegiance. RB was a convinced Baptist. He was critical of the Baptist Union but remained within it throughout his life. It would have been better, perhaps, for him either to have taken an active role in the activity of the Union, or to have left it to follow his own vision. According to his son, there was some tension in his father's thinking:

My father's position amongst that section of Baptists who sought to meet the present tendencies in the Union was, I suppose, that of generally accepted leader. This was certainly true of him as regards every denomination in Wales, and very probably in the Baptist Union of Great Britain. His attitude was rapidly changing during the last few months of his life, and he was becoming inclined to the opinion that the only course was secession.[36]

W. S. Jones, Nantlais Williams and Keri Evans, although kindred spirits, were more committed to their respective denominations.

Nantlais commemorated R. B. Jones's life and contribution in a brief poem that has been translated by J. R. Morgan:

The Prophet of the Holy Scriptures

Thou didst climb the solitary tracks,
  The paths by which the shepherds go;
On mountain sides, o'er perilous brakes,
  Ne'er given common foot to know.

Thy soul burned hot in passionate search,
  Thyself wert lost to us oft time;
Whilst we in restful ease did watch
  The fold and the ninety and nine.

Truly thou did'st bleed from wounds received,
  Yet these thou would'st not sadly mourn,
Thy friends erstwhile who narrowly perceived
  Might thus discern the marks of thorn.

Through the land thine insistent cry was heard,
  Thou the prophet of the Precious Blood,
But those lips today speak not a word;
  The shepherd is at home with God.[37]

RB was a man of the Bible, loving his Bible because he found the Lord Jesus Christ in it. The bond between himself and his Saviour was such that he was deeply moved when thinking and speaking of him. The passion in RB's preaching reflected his passion for the Lord Jesus Christ.

Owen Thomas, a former student at Porth, went to see him during his last illness. When he was leaving, RB looked at him and said three times, 'I love Jesus Christ.'[38] Let us leave him with his Saviour.

Notes

Chapter 1

1. For the Guest family: *Dictionary of Welsh Biography* (1959) [henceforth *DWB*].
2. J. Ronald Williams and Gwyneth Williams, *History of Caersalem, Dowlais* (Gomerian Press, 1967), 136; 'Corfforiad Hebron, Dowlais', *Y Bedyddiwr*, July 1846.
3. Ieuan Gwynedd Jones, 'The Merthyr of Henry Richard', *Merthyr Politics: A Working Class Tradition*, ed. Glanmor Williams (Cardiff, 1966), 49.
4. Census Returns, 1871.
5. *Merthyr Tydfil, A Valley Community* (Merthyr Teachers' Centre Group, 1981), 425.
6. Robert V. Barnes, 'A History of the Railways of Merthyr Tydfil', *Merthyr Historian*, vol. 1, 1976.
7. *Merthyr Tydfil, A Valley Community*, 369.
8. Copy of birth certificate, Registrar General, Merthyr Tydfil. For some reason, Ithel Jones gives the year as 1870, 'R. B. Jones, Porth', *Seren Gomer*, September 1939.
9. Census Returns, 1871.
10. Ibid.
11. Glanmor Williams, *A Life* (2002), 11.
12. The father was baptised in 1859; married Mary, daughter of Job Bevan, 1868; made deacon in 1877 and secretary in 1884: 'John Jones, Hebron, Dowlais', *Yr Hauwr*, December 1902.
13. Geraint Jones, 'RB (By His Son)', *Seren Cymru*, 2 July 1943; Brynmor Pierce Jones, *The King's Champions* (Rev. B. P. Jones, 1986 ed.), 13.
14. Robert V. Barnes, *The Merthyr Historian*, vol. 1, 1976, 60.
15. Ithel Jones, *Seren Gomer*, September 1939; Brynmor Pierce Jones, *The King's Champions*, 13.
16. Leslie Wynne Evans, *Education in Industrial Wales* (Leslie Wynne Evans, 1971), 96 (2).

17. 'It was most certainly her inspiration and vision that called into being the extensive and highly successful and popular evening schools which were the consummation of an elaborate educational system': Leslie Wynne Evans, *Education in Industrial Wales*, 99, 104.
18. Ibid., 97, 296.
19. Ibid., 98.
20. Brynmor Pierce Jones, *The King's Champions*, 14; Geraint Jones, 'R. B. Jones (By His Son)', *Seren Cymru*, 26 July 1943, the third article in a series; William Joseph Rhys, *Braslun o Hanes Salem, Porth, Cwm Rhondda* (Aberdare, n.d.), 38.
21. Ithel Jones, *Seren Gomer*, September 1939.
22. Geraint Jones, 'R. B. Jones (By His Son)', *Seren Cymru*, 26 July 1943, the second article; Owen Waldo James (1845–1910); he was from Llanfachreth, Anglesey; ministered at Cwmafan and Dowlais. His wife Ellen was from Penydarren, *Yr Hauwr*, May 1896; *Llawlyfr y Bedyddwyr*, 1911.
23. *Merthyr Tydfil, A Valley Community*, 162, 418.
24. Brynmor Pierce Jones, *The King's Champions*, 14.
25. Ibid.
26. William Edwards (1848–1929), DWB.
27. Glanmor Williams: *A Life*, 11. For Ceinfryn Thomas: *Yr Hauwr*, July 1896; *Llawlyfr y Bedyddwyr*, 1920.
28. Geraint Jones, *Seren Cymru*, 26 July 1943.
29. Brynmor Pierce Jones, *The King's Champions*, 16.
30. Ibid., 16.
31. Brynmor Pierce Jones, 'A Biographical Study of the Rev. R. B. Jones (1869–1933), First Principal of the South Wales Bible Institute, with A critical Survey of Welsh Fundamentalism in the post-revival era.' Thesis, 1966. Copy at Wales Evangelical School of Theology, Bryntirion, Bridgend.
32. NLW, R. B. Jones Papers, Minor Collections, No. 3; sermon on Isaiah 55:10-11, preached at Berth-lwyd, 3 January 1894.
33. Brynmor Pierce Jones, *The King's Champions*, 17, but she was from Cwmafan and not Aberafan: 'Llewelyn Griffith, Cwmavon', *Yr Hauwr*, August 1899.
34. NLW, Caersalem Collection (1892–1976), No. 2. Copy of the call, 21 January 1895, in R. B. Jones Papers, Minor Collections, No.1.
35. Ibid., Caersalem Collection (2).

36. 'Undeb Bedyddwyr Llanelli a'r Cylch', *Llanelli Mercury*, 18 April 1895.
37. 'Caersalem, Llanelli', *Llanelli Mercury*, 16 May 1895.
38. John Rhys Morgan (1822–1900), *DWB*.
39. John Rowlands (1825–1909), *Llawlyfr y Bedyddwyr*, 1910.
40. For the Llanelli ministers: Gwilym Rees, *Cofiant y Parch. Thomas Johns, D.D.* (Llanelli, 1929); John Thomas, *Hanes Eglwysi Annibynol Cymru, V* (Dolgellau, 1891), 359; *Coflyfr y Dathliad, 1875–1925, Y Tabernacl, Llanelli* (1925), 19, and photograph of D. Wynne Evans. From Llanelli he moved to Chester, and then to London.
41. *Seren Gomer*, 1935, 97-101; Nantlais, 'Marw W.S', *Y Cymro*, 10 September 1933; three memorial articles in *Yr Efengylydd*, September 1933; 'Y Diweddar Barch. W. S. Jones, Llwynypia', *Seren Gomer*, 1935; Geraint Jones, 'Y Parch. W. S. Jones Yng Ngoleuni ei Lythyrau at y Parch. R. B. Jones', *Seren Cymru*, 4, 11 April 1947; 'W. S. Jones', in Robert Ellis, *Living Echoes of the Welsh Revival* (London, 1951).
42. *Llawlyfr Undeb Bedyddwyr Cymru* (1969), 32.
43. NLW, Caersalem Collection, Church Minutes, 20 January 1895.
44. Ibid., 3 August 1895.
45. Ibid., 17 April 1896.
46. Ibid., 9 May 1895.
47. Ibid., 17 April 1896.
48. 'Undeb Bedyddwyr Llanelli a'r Cylch', *Seren Cymru*, 4 July 1895.
49. NLW, Caersalem Collection, Church Minutes, 3 August 1895; 2 December 1895; 12 December 1897; 'Caersalem, Llanelli', *Seren Cymru*, 25 July 1895.
50. Brynmor Pierce Jones, *The King's Champions*, 17-18. When, later, RB used the book at Salem, Porth, it was the translation by John Rhys Morgan (*Lleurwg*): *Braslun o Hanes Eglwys Salem*, 22.
51. NLW, Caersalem Collection, Church Minutes, 25 October 1895, 3 August 1895.
52. Geraint Jones, *Seren Cymru*, 6 August 1943.
53. NLW, R. B. Jones Papers, Minor Collections, No. 1.
54. Ibid.
55. Ibid.
56. Copy of the call, 9 July 1899, R. B. Jones Papers, Minor Collections, No.1.

57. Ibid., J & A Jones to Rhys & Co, 13 July 1899.
58. Ibid., the call, 9 July 1899.

Chapter 2

1. William Joseph Rhys, *Braslun o Hanes Eglwys Salem Porth* (Aberdare, n.d.), 16; *Undeb Bedyddwyr Cymru a Mynwy, Llawlyfr Salem Porth, 1931* (Tonypandy, 1931); NLW, R. B. Jones Papers, Minor Collections, No. 1.
2. For the background: E. D. Lewis, 'Population changes and social life, 1860–1914', Ceri W. Lewis, 'The Welsh Languge', in E. D. Lewis, *Rhondda Past and Present,* ed. K. Hopkins (1975).
3. Charles Preece, *Woman of the Valleys* (second edition, 1989), 125.
4. 'Mr Evans became his friend, adviser and often a generous bene-factor in later years', Brynmor Pierce Jones, *The King's Champions*, 50. William Evans was born in Fishguard, one of fourteen children, and came to work in the Rhondda. He owned Thomas and Evans, Grocers, in Hannah Street, and also Hill's Works, producing Corona pop. It is now a television and record-ing studio. William Evans gave Bronwydd Park and the Public Library to Porth. For William Evans: Owen Vernon Jones, *William Evans* (Porth Comprehensive School, n.d.), especially the chapter 'Public Servant and Christian Philanthropist'.
5. *Braslun o Hanes Eglwys Salem,* 19, 22.
6. Church Minutes, Hebron, Dowlais, 4 December 1899.
7. Brynmor Pierce Jones, *The King's Champions*, 19-20; Brynmor P. Jones comments on RB's organising ability, the 'immaculate, mil-itary planning of the Annual Meetings at Salem', Thesis, 48.
8. Rhondda Churches web site.
9. Brynmor Pierce Jones, *The King's Champions*, 20.
10. R. B. Jones, *Rent Heavens* (London, 1931), 30.
11. Noel Gibbard, *Fire on the Altar* (Bryntirion Press, 2002), 35.
12. J. Rhys Davies, 'To God Be the Glory', *Yr Efengylydd*, September 1923; D. Wynne Evans, 'Er cof am y diweddar Barch. J. Rhys Davies', *Yr Efengylydd*, May 1926.
13. Ibid., D. Wynne Evans, *Yr Efengylydd*, 1926.
14. 'Recollections and Reflections', *Yr Efengylydd*, May 1923.
15. 'The visit of Mr Meyer last summer at the invitation of F.C.C. has helped to this', J. Rhys Davies to H. D. Phillips, 11 November 1902,

NLW, Brynmor P. Jones, Research Papers, Minor Collections, No. 19.
16. Noel Gibbard, *Fire on the Altar*, 24.
17. W. S. Jones, 'The Rev. R. B. Jones, Preacher and Minister', *Witness and a Minister*, 1933.
18. NLW, R. B. Jones Papers, Minor Collections, No. 1, W. S. Jones to R. B. Jones, 20 July 1903.
19. Brynmor P. Jones, Thesis; *Yr Efengylydd*, xxv, 85, 86.
20. NLW, R. B. Jones Papers, Minor Collections, No. 1, letter 15 April 1903.
21. R. B. Jones, *Rent Heavens*, 31.
22. Ministers: 'Y Diweddar Barch. E. Gwynhefin Thomas', *Yr Efengylydd*, February 1933; R. S. Morris (1867–1933), born in Holyhead (the family then moving to Porthmadog), had a long ministry at Penuel, Cwmafan, 1894–1925, *Llawlyfr y Bedyddwyr*, 1934; James Nicholas (1877–1963) ministered at Tonypandy 1901–1915, welcomed the Revival 1904, and also spoke in public meetings supporting Keir Hardie, *Llawlyfr y Bedyddwyr*, 1964; W. Cynog Williams (1868–1941), born in Llangynog, Carmarthenshire, ministered at Cilfowyr and Ramoth, Pembrokeshire, before moving to Heolyfelin in 1901 and staying there until 1941, *Llawlyfr y Bedyddwyr*, 1943; Nantlais, 'Cynog', *Yr Efengylydd*, July 1941, ibid. T. E. Thomas, 'Y Parch. W. Cynog Williams'.
23. Brynmor Pierce Jones, *The Spiritual History of Keswick in Wales* (Cwmbran, Gwent, 1989), 11.
24. *Yr Efengylydd*, 1933.
25. Brynmor Pierce Jones, *The King's Champions*, 49.
26. Brynmor P. Jones, *Voices from the Welsh Revival, 1904–1905* (Evangelical Press of Wales, 1995), 14, 15; O. M. Owen, 'Atgofion o'i Bererindod Ysbrydol', *Yr Efengylydd*, 1933.
27. 'Atgofion o'i Bererindod Ysbrydol', *Yr Efengylydd*, 1933.
28. Brynmor Pierce Jones, *The King's Champions*, 49; other examples: Brynmor P. Jones, *Voices from the Welsh Revival 1904–1905* (Evangelical Press of Wales, 1995), 14-15.
29. 'Salem, Porth', *Seren Cymru*, 20 January 1905.
30. R. B. Jones, *Rent Heavens*, 32.
31. Ibid., 33.
32. Ibid., 34.
33. Noel Gibbard, *Fire on the Altar*, 36, 73, 76; idem, *Caniadau'r Diwygiad*, 61-2.

34. Brynmor P. Jones, Thesis, 74-5.
35. Letters in *The Rhondda Leader*, 11, 18 June 1904; 'At y Golygydd', 25 June 1904. See next chapter, reference 71.
36. *Braslun o Hanes Eglwys Salem*, 20.
37. W. S. Jones, 'The Rev. R. B. Jones, Preacher and Minister', *A Witness and a Minister*, 1933.
38. Noel Gibbard, *Fire on the Altar,* 37.
39. Ibid.
40. 'Llwynypia', *The Rhondda Leader*, 26 November 1904.
41. 'RB (By His Son)', *Seren Cymru*, 27 August 1943.
42. 'Upper Rhondda Welsh Baptists', *The Rhondda Leader*, 4 June 1904; NLW 22856D.
43. NLW 22856D; 'Ymweliad Emlyn Davies', *The Rhondda Leader*, 4 June 1904.
44. Ibid.
45. NLW 22856D.
46. Brynmor Pierce Jones, *Spiritual History*, 13.
47. Copy of the call, NLW, R. B. Jones Papers, Minor Collections, No. 1.
48. Brynmor P. Jones, Thesis, 139.
49. NLW, R. B. Jones Papers, Minor Collections, No. 1, letter 16, August 1904.
50. Ibid., 13 July 1904.
51. Ibid.
52. Ibid.
53. 'RB (By His Son)', *Seren Cymru*, 10 September 1943; sixth in a series of articles.
54. Ibid.
55. NLW, R. B. Jones Papers, Minor Collections; list of engagements, No. 9.
56. Ibid., R. B. Jones Papers, Minor Collections, No. 1, Cynog Williams to R. B. Jones, 2 December 1904.
57. Ibid.
58. Hebron, Dowlais, Church Minutes, 28 August, 19 September, 12 October 1904.
59. 'Hebron Chapel Revival', *The Merthyr Express*, 8, 15 October 1904; 'Nodweddion y Diwygiad', *Seren Cymru,* 16 December 1904. A large number left Hebron during 1906–7; a high number left without 'a letter'; a good number were 'dismissed', and many

were holding services in their homes, rather than in the chapel, Hebron Church Minutes, 'Account of changes 1906'; meeting 9 October 1907.

60. 'Y Diwygiwr yn Heolyfelin, Aberdar', *Tarian y Gweithiwr*, 29 December 1904.

61. NLW 22856D.

62. 'RB (By His Son)', *Seren Cymru*, 13 August 1943.

63. *A Witness and a Minister*, 1933.

64. Rosina Davies, *The Story of My Life* (Llandysul, 1942), 185.

65. W. S. Jones, *Y Diwygiad Crefyddol yn Rhosllanerchrugog,* 1904-5 (from the Rhos *Herald*), 3; Evan Williams, 'Hanes Dechreuad y Diwygiad yn Rhosllannerchrugog', *Yr Efengylydd*, February 1936.

66. Evan Williams, 'Hanes Dechreuad y Diwygiad'.

67. Evan Williams (1863–1939). He was born in Bethesda, Gwynedd, and educated at Llangollen and Bangor. He ministered at Penuel, Rhos, from 1894 until 1911: *Llawlyfr y Bedyddwyr*, 1940.

68. O. M. Owen, 'Rev. R. B. Jones—A Revival Flame', *A Witness and a Minister*, 1933.

69. Based on: Lewis Valentine, *Hanes Penuel Rhosllannerchrugog* (Llandysul, 1959); W. S. Jones, *Y Diwygiad Crefyddol yn Rhosllanerchrugog* (1905); Evan Williams, 'Hanes Dechreuad y Diwygiad', *Yr Efengylydd*, February 1936; Christian Worker, 'Diwygiad 1904-5 yn Rhosllanerchrugog', *Yr Efengylydd*, March, April 1933; 'Adfywiad yn y Rhos', *Yr Herald Cymraeg,* 22 November 1904, 'Rhos', *Wrexham Advertiser*, 26 November 1904.

70. Evan Williams' second article, *Yr Efengylydd*, May 1936.

Chapter 3

1. 'Pentre, Rhondda', *The Rhondda Leader*, 12 November 1904.

2. Ibid., 'Llwynypia', 26 November 1904.

3. Ibid., 'The Revival at Ynyshir', 10 December 1904.

4. 'Y Diwygiad', *Seren Cymru*, 16 December 1904.

5. 'The Revival at Ynyshir', *The Rhondda Leader*, 10 December 1904.

6. Awstin, *Religious Revival in Wales*, No. 1, 28 November 1904.

7. 'Revival Baptism at Salem Porth', *Pontypridd Chronicle*, 17 December 1904.

8. 'Noddfa, Pontygwaith', *Seren Cymru*, 17 February 1905.

9. D. Hopkin, 'R. B. Jones', *Seren Cymru*, 22 September 1939.
10. NLW, Brynmor P. Jones Research Papers, Minor Collections, No. 33, Rhys B. Jones to Mrs Penn-Lewis, 10 January 1905.
11. Ibid.
12. Ibid.
13. R. Tudur Jones mentions them by name: *Tân ar yr Ynys*, ed. Geraint Tudur (Gwasg Gwynedd, 2004), 19-20, 29.
14. Noel Gibbard, *Fire on the Altar*, 72, 73.
15. NLW, Brynmor P. Jones Research Papers, Minor Collections, No. 33, Rhys B. Jones to Mrs Penn-Lewis, 10 January 1905.
16. Ibid.
17. Ibid.
18. Ibid.
19. *Tân ar yr Ynys*, 20.
20. NLW, Brynmor P. Jones Research Papers, Minor Collections, No. 33, Rhys B. Jones to Mrs Penn-Lewis, 10 January 1905.
21. Ibid.
22. 'R. B. Jones yn Llanfachreth a'r cylch', *Seren Cymru*, 10 February 1905.
23. Ibid.
24. 'Y Diwygiad', *Yr Herald Cymraeg*, 10 February 1905.
25. *Seren Cymru*, 10 February 1905.
26. *Seren Cymru*, 26 January 1905; Brynmor P. Jones, *Voices from the Welsh Revival*, 106-7.
27. Brynmor P. Jones, *Voices from the Welsh Revival*, 107
28. Brynmor P. Jones, *Voices from the Welsh Revival*, 107. Some of the students mentioned by name: John Thomas Phillips, Thomas Bassett, Evan Williams, Morgan Jones, D. C. Griffiths, and W. J. Rees: Brynmor P. Jones, *Voices from the Welsh Revival*, 106; *Tân ar yr Ynys*, 22; D. Hopkin, *Seren Cymru*, 22 September 1939.
29. D. Hopkin, *Seren Cymru*, 'R. B. Jones', 22 September 1939.
30. Jessie Penn-Lewis, *The Awakening in Wales* (Overcomer Publications, n.d.), 62; R. B. Jones, *Rent Heavens*, 44-5.
31. Brynmor Pierce Jones, *The King's Champions*, 71.
32. R. B. Jones, *Rent Heavens*, 44-5. Another person was probably referring to this event. The congregation was in a 'heavenly swoon' ('*llesmair nefol*'), and stamped the floor lightly as an accompaniment to the preaching: D. Hopkin, 'R. B. Jones', *Seren Cymru*, 22 September 1939.

33. Noel Gibbard, *Fire on the Altar*, 73.
34. 'Y Diwygiad', *Yr Herald Cymraeg*, 7 February 1905.
35. Report in the *Welsh Gazette*, 9 February 1905.
36. 'Two hundred converts', *North Wales Guardian*, 20 January 1905.
37. 'Caernarfon', *Yr Herald Cymraeg*, 7 March 1905.
38. 'The Religious Revival', *Carnarvon and Denbigh Herald*; 3 March 1905; 'Caernarfon', *Yr Herald Cymraeg,* 9 March 1905.
39. 'The Religious Revival', *Carnarvon and Denbigh Herald,* 3 March 1905.
40. Ibid.
41. Ibid.
42. 'Y Diwygiad', *Seren Cymru*, 14 April 1905.
43. 'Y Diwygiad', *Yr Herald Cymraeg*, 7, 14 March 1905.
44. NLW, R. B. Jones Papers, Minor Collections, No. 9, list of engagements.
45. 'Corwen', *Wrexham Advertiser*, 15 April 1905.
46. 'Dyddiaduron Cernyw', *Trafodion Cymdeithas Hanes y Bedyddwyr*, 1970, 30.
47. *Tân ar yr Ynys*, 23.
48. NLW, Brynmor P. Jones Research Papers, Minor Collections Jones Papers, No. 33, letter, 15 April 1905.
49. Ibid.
50. Ibid., letter, 25 April 1905.
51. Ibid.
52. Ibid.
53. NLW, R. B. Jones Papers, Minor Collections, No. 9, list of engagements.
54. Noel Gibbard, *Caniadau'r Diwygiad*, 74.
55. 'Dinbych', *Seren Cymru*, 4 August 1905.
56. NLW, R. B. Jones Papers, Minor Collections, No. 33, Rhys B. Jones to Mrs Penn-Lewis, 16:9:05.
57. Ibid.
58. Ibid.
59. Ibid., Rhys B. Jones to Mrs Penn-Lewis, 3:10:05
60. Ibid.
61. Ibid.
62. Noel Gibbard, *Fire on the Altar*, 182-3.
63. NLW, R. B. Jones Papers, Minor Collections, No. 9; list of engagements.

64. 'Y Parch. R. B. Jones yn Siloh, Tredegar', *Seren Cymru*, 20 October 1905.
65. Brynmor P. Jones, Thesis, 106.
66. NLW, R. B. Jones Papers, Minor Collections, No. 9, list of engagements.
67. 'Ymweliad Mr. Evan Roberts a Tonyrefail', *Y Goleuad*, 15 December 1905.
68. 'Bethesda, Abercwmboi', *Seren Cymru*, 13 April 1906.
69. Ibid., 'Yma ac Acw', 20 April 1906.
70. Ibid., 'Amlwch', 15 June 1906.
71. Full account: 'The Trouble at Jerusalem, Llwynypia', *Y Darian*, 21 June 1906.
72. Ibid.
73. R. B. Jones, *Rent Heavens*, 29.
74. Noel Gibbard, *Fire on the Altar*, 54-5, 126.
75. Brynmor P. Jones, Thesis, 125.
76. NLW, Brynmor P. Jones Research Papers, Minor Collections, No. 19, JPL to Mr Head, 20 February 1905; copy of the letter not signed.
77. Ibid., No. 3, 1 February 1905.
78. Ibid., 20 February 1905
79. Ibid., No. 2, 11 April 1905.
80. Ibid., letter to 'Granine', 21 January 1905.
81. Ibid.; No. 19, to Dr Pierson, 1 March 1905.
82. Ibid.
83. Ibid., O. M. Owen to Mrs Penn-Lewis, n.d.
84. Ibid., letter, not signed, 31 January 1905.
85. No. 33, 7 April 1905.
86. Ibid., R. B. Jones to JPL, 15 April 1905.
87. Ibid.
88. Ibid., No. 4, Jessie Penn-Lewis to Mr Jones, 25 April 1905.
89. Ibid., No. 33, 7 April 1905.
90. 'The Awakening in Wales and Elsewhere', *The Life of Faith*, 12 July 1905.
91. 'RB', *Seren Cymru*, 28 April 1933.
92. NLW, Brynmor P. Jones Research Papers, No. 20.
93. Brynmor Pierce Jones, *The Trials and Triumphs of Mrs. Jessie Penn-Lewis* (Bridge–Logos Publishers, 1997), 149.
94. 'Yma ac Acw', *Seren Cymru*, 13 April 1906.
95. Ibid., 18.

96. R. B. Jones Papers, Minor Collections, No. 4, 7 September 1906.
97. Brynmor P. Jones, Thesis, 127.
98. Ibid.

Chapter 4
1. Brynmor P. Jones, Thesis, 140-1.
2. John Thomas Phillips (1876–1945): *Llawlyfr y Bedyddwyr*, 1946.
3. NLW, Brynmor P. Jones, Research Papers, Minor Collections, No. 33.
4. Ibid. Brynmor P. Jones discusses the Ainon ministry, Thesis, 138-48.
5. NLW, R. B. Jones Papers, Minor collections, E. Tudno Jones, 'The Ministry of the Rev. R. B. Jones at Ainon, Ynyshir', No. 35, 10. E. Tudno Jones contributed other articles on RB: Tudno Jones, 'Atgofion am y Parchedig R. B. Jones', *Yr Efengylydd*, 31 (*sic*, 32), November 1941; Emlyn Tudno Jones, 'Y Rhai sydd ynom', *Seren Gomer*, Summer, 1961.
6. Ibid., 11.
7. Ibid., 9-10.
8. Ibid., 10; Brynmor Pierce Jones, *The King's Champions*, 118.
9. NLW, R. B. Jones Papers, Minor Collections, E. Tudno Jones, 'The Ministry of the Rev. R. B. Jones', No. 35.
10. Ibid.
11. Noel Gibbard, *On the Wings of the Dove*, 80-3.
12. Ibid., 83-4.
13. NLW, R. B. Jones Papers, Minor Collections, No. 4, letter 29 January 1904.
14. Ibid., No. 1, letter 9 February 1904; W. S. Jones, writing to RB in America, referred to a meeting that was held at Ainon. He knew that in the past he had known 'flint' there, but 'The heart I saw last night had no flint in it', ibid., letter 19 April 1907, No. 1; included in RB's reading during the journey were the works of Madam Guyon (also an influence on Mrs Penn-Lewis), ibid., W. S. Jones to RB, 23 February 1907.
15. L. Ton Evans ('Junius'): T. M. Bassett and S. H. Olsen, 'Lewis Ton Evans (Junius)', *Trafodion Cymdeithas Hanes y Bedyddwyr*, 1993.
16. Brynmor Pierce Jones, *The King's Champions*, 77.
17. Noel Gibbard, *On the Wings of the Dove*, 75-6.
18. Ibid., 85.

19. Ibid., 84-5.
20. Ibid., 85.
21. Ibid.
22. NLW, Brynmor P. Jones, Research Papers, Minor Collections, No. 30.
23. Ibid.
24. Noel Gibbard, *On the Wings of the Dove*, 85-6.
25. NLW, R. B. Jones Papers, Minor Collections, No.1, W. J. Nicholas to R. B. Jones, 7 August 1907.
26. Ibid.
27. Ibid., R. B. Jones Papers, No. 4.
28. Ibid.
29. Brynmor Pierce Jones, *The King's Champions*, 78.
30. Ibid.
31. Ibid.
32. *Llyfryn Coffa, Ainon, Ynyshir, 1880–1914*, 11.
33. Ibid., 12.
34. Brynmor Pierce Jones, *The King's Champions*, 119.
35. Ibid., 116.
36. Ibid., 119; *Llyfryn Coffa*, 12, 14.
37. *Llyfryn Coffa*, 12.
38. O. M. Owen, 'Rev. R. B. Jones—A Revival Flame', *A Witness and a Minister*, Memorial Number, 1933.
39. Noel Gibbard, *On the Wings of the Dove*, 215; T. M. Bassett, *The Baptists of Wales and the Baptist Missionary Society* (Swansea, 1991), 67.
40. *Llyfryn Coffa*, 15-16.
41. 'The story of what led to the Schools' inception', *A Witness and a Minister*, August 1925.
42. Ibid.
43. Ibid.
44. Ibid.
45. Ibid.
46. For the first three ministers: *DWB* (1959) and John Morgan Jones *DWB* (1970).

Chapter 5

1. NLW, Brynmor P. Jones, Research Papers, Minor Collections, 'Announcement', No. 20.

2. Report in Brynmor P. Jones Research Papers, Minor Collections, No. 3.
3. Ibid.
4. Ibid., letter 8 January 1909.
5. Ibid.
6. Noel Gibbard, *On the Wings of the Dove*, 134, 151.
7. NLW, Brynmor P. Jones Research Papers, Minor Collections, 'Convention of the Message of the Cross', No. 14.
8. Ibid.
9. Ibid.; Brynmor Pierce Jones, *The King's Champions*, 126.
10. Brynmor Pierce Jones, *The Spiritual History*, 21-2.
11. 'Cynadledd Hynod', *Yr Efengylydd*, March 1913; the year was 1913 and not 1914 as mentioned by Brynmor Pierce Jones, *The King's Champions*, 162.
12. *Yr Efengylydd*, March 1913.
13. J. D. Williams, *Cynhadledd y Sulgwyn, Rhydaman, 1917–1967* (1967), 9-10.
14. Ibid.
15. Ibid., 10.
16. Ibid., 13.
17. Ibid., 11-12.
18. Ibid., 15-16.
19. Ibid., 16.
20. Ibid., 17.
21. Ibid.
22. Hebron, Dowlais, Church Minutes, 11 August 1908.
23. 'Cenadaethau, Cynadleddau', *Yr Efengylydd*, January 1909.
24. Brynmor Pierce Jones, *The King's Champions*, 97-8; 'Milwr Da i Iesu Grist', *Yr Efengylydd*, 1933.
25. 'Milwr Da i Iesu Grist' *Yr Efengylydd*, 1933; also, Goronwy Prys Owen, 'Llenyddiaeth y Diwygiad', in *Nefol Dan*, ed. Noel Gibbard.
26. Brynmor Pierce Jones, *The King's Champions*, 246-7. 'In 1908 the Dover Directory lists Mrs Beresford Baker with a House of Rest at 11 and 12 Princes Street (and her husband Captain Beresford Baker living separately at 25 Waterloo Crescent)', Website, History of the PWSTS Building.
27. NLW, R. B. Jones Papers, Minor Collections, No. 1, DS (D. S. Jones) to RB, 2 October 1907.

28. E.g. David Jones, November 1909; Henry Rees, February 1912; Daniel Thomas, January 1912; Watkin Roberts, April 1913, Rees Howells, February, March 1916.
29. 'Cerbyd yr Efengylydd', *Yr Efengylydd*, July 1909.
30. Ibid., July and August.
31. Editorial, *Yr Efengylydd*, September 1909.
32. Ibid.
33. Ibid.; 'Cerbyd yr Efengylydd'.
34. 'Cerbyd yr Efengylydd', *Yr Efengylydd*, September, October 1909.
35. 'Cerbyd yr Efengylydd', *Yr Efengylydd*, July 1910.
36. Brynmor Pierce Jones, *The King's Champions*, 109.
37. 'Neuadd Genadol Newydd', *Yr Efengylydd*, December 1913.
38. Ibid., 'Cerbyd yr Efengylydd', June 1913.
39. Ibid., July 1913.
40. Ibid., August 1913.
41. Ibid., September 1913.
42. Ibid., October 1913.
43. Ibid., 'Darfu'r Haf, Beth am y Gaeaf?', October 1912.
44. Ibid., November 1912.
45. Ibid., 'Y Babell Genadol', December 1913.
46. Ibid., 'Cenhadaeth Gartrefol yr Efengylydd', May 1914.
47. Brynmor Pierce Jones, *The King's Champions*, 112-13.
48. Ibid., 112; 'Ein Cenhadaeth Gartrefol, *Yr Efengylydd*, July 1915, January 1916.
49. Ibid., 'Cenhadaeth Gartrefol Yr Efengylydd', December 1915.
50. NLW, R. B. Jones Papers, Minor Collections, No. 1.
51. 'Tit-Bits', *Porth Gazette*, 8 November 1919.
52. Ibid.

Chapter 6
1. *The Tabernacle Porth, Jubilee Souvenir*, 1874–1924, 2.
2. Rhondda Churches web site
3. Howell Williams, *The Romance of the Forward Movement* (Davies Lecture, 1946), 101.
4. *Jubilee Souvenir*, 7. A vestry had been built in 1875, ibid., 5.
5. Ibid., 6
6. Ibid., 8.
7. Ibid., 9.

8. Ibid., 13-17.
9. Ibid., 18.
10. Ibid., 18-20.
11. Ibid., 21.
12. Ibid., 22.
13. 'Tit-Bits', *Porth Gazette*, 13, 20 December 1919.
14. *Jubilee Souvenir*, 21-2.
15. Ibid., 22.
16. Ibid., 28
17. Brynmor P. Jones, Thesis, 358.
18. Brynmor Pierce Jones, *The King's Champions*, 189.
19. Ibid., 182.
20. Copy: NLW, R. B. Jones Papers, Minor Collections, No. 8.
21. Ibid.
22. Brynmor Pierce Jones, *The King's Champions*, 183.
23. Ibid., 181.
24. *The Children's Bible School* (catechism); personal copy.
25. Ibid.
26. Ibid.
27. Pryse Lewis, 'A Witness and a Minister', *Yr Efengylydd*, 1933. 'The condition of membership, punctuality, regularity at services and bringing of Bible and Hymn-book', *Church Manual and Record*, 1929.
28. *Church Manual and Record*, 1924, 1926, 1927.
29. Personal copy; copy in NLW, R. B. Jones Papers, Minor Collections, No. 9; Brynmor Pierce Jones, *The King's Champions*, 192-3; *Church Manual and Record*, 1926, 1928.
30. E.g. *Church Manual and Record*, 1926.
31. NLW, R. B. Jones Papers, Minor Collections, No. 14.
32. Ibid.
33. Ibid.
34. Ibid.
35. RB sent a copy of the published work to Evan Roberts and he sent a letter of thanks to the author: *Yr Efengylydd*, April 1926.
36. 'Diferion o'r Gynhadledd', *Yr Efengylydd*, September 1926.
37. Brynmor Pierce Jones, *The King's Champions*, 190; *Jubilee Souvenir*, 27.
38. Brynmor Pierce Jones, *The King's Champions*, 191.
39. 'Y Genhadaeth Gartrefol', *Yr Efengylydd*, June 1922.

40. Ibid., July–August 1920.
41. RB was still co-editor. Brynmor Pierce Jones refers to Nantlais and T. R. Williams as 'new editors', *The King's Champions*, 148. This is misleading; T. R. Williams joined RB and Nantlais. T. R. Williams (1881–1972), *Llawlyfr y Bedyddwyr*, 1973.
42. Noel Gibbard, *On the Wings of the Dove*, 195-6.
43. Ibid.
44. Examples: Watkin Roberts, 'Brwydr y Beibl', *Yr Efengylydd*, February, May 1923; ibid., John Thomas, 'Y Feirniadaeth Ddinistriol a'r Ysgrythurau', series April to December 1924.
45. J. Cynog Williams, 'Beibl a Beirniadaeth', *Seren Cymru*; R. B. Jones, 'Mwy o Oleuni', 9 March 1923; ibid., 'Mwy o Oleuni', 16 March 1923. Examples of support for RB: D. W. Davies, 'Beibl a Beirniadaeth', 30 March 1923; letter, 'At un o'r Uwchfeirniaid', 25 May 1923; criticisms of RB: Thomas Lewis, 'Mwy o Oleuni', 23 March 1923; 'Ein Cenhadon', 6 April 1923; W. H. Pritchard. 'Dysgu'r Genhadaeth', 13 April 1923.
46. Ibid., 'Cyhuddiadau Cyhuddwyr y Cenhadon', 15 June 1923.
47. Ibid.
48. 'Cyhuddiadau Cyhuddwyr y Cenhadon', 21 September 1923. There were two further replies to RB, 12, 19 October, and he responded, 2 November.
49. There is a helpful discussion by Brian Stanley: *The History of the Baptist Missionary Society*, 1792–1992 (Edinburgh, 1992), 277-83, 377-81.
50. *Jubilee Souvenir*, 23.
51. Noel Gibbard, *On the Wings of the Dove*, 217-19.
52. The intention was to open a Bible school in Calcutta, and not Assam, as Brynmor Pierce Jones says: *The King's Champions*, 174.
53. Noel Gibbard, *On the Wings of the Dove*, 134, 137.
54. 'Taith y Parch R. B. Jones yn America', *Yr Efengylydd*, July 1923. They arrived in May, not June, as Brynmor Pierce Jones says: *The King's Champions*, 174.
55. *Yr Efengylydd*, July 1923.
56. Ibid.
57. Ibid.
58. Ibid., September 1923.
59. Ibid.

60. NLW, R. B. Jones Papers, Minor Collections, No. 36.
61. Typed account of 'Fifty Years in the Christian Ministry', personal copy.
62. Ibid.; *Church Manual and Record,* 1926, 1927.
63. Brynmor Pierce Jones, *The King's Champions*, 113-14.
64. 'Cenhadaeth Gartrefol y Tabernacl, Porth', *Yr Efengylydd*, August 1928.
65. 'I Riga ac yn ol', *Yr Efengylydd*, March 1927.
66. Ibid., April 1927.
67. Ibid., June 1927.
68. Ibid., January 1928.
69. Ibid., February 1928.
70. Ibid., May 1928.
71. Ibid., 'Dros Dir a Mor', March 1927; the whole work was finished a little later, and meetings held on 7 August 1927, 'Dros Dir a Mor', *Yr Efengylydd*, August 1927.
72. Ibid., 'I Riga ac yn ol', May 1928.
73. Ibid., 'Dros Dir a Mor', November 1927.
74. Ibid., October 1927.
75. Brynmor Pierce Jones, *The King's Champions*, 173.
76. 'Keswick Canada', *Yr Efengylydd*, September 1928.
77. Ibid., 'Tro Arall Tros y Werydd', *Yr Efengylydd*, October 1928.
78. Brynmor Pierce Jones, *The King's Champions*, 194-5.
79. Brynmor P. Jones, Thesis, 357, and other examples of criticisms, 355-7.
80. Brynmor Pierce Jones, *The King's Champions*, 193-4.

Chapter 7

1. 'The Bible Training School for Christian Workers', *Yr Efengylydd*, December 1919; 'The Story of what led to the School's Inception', *A Witness and a Minister*, 1925; 'Founder and First Principal of the South Wales Bible Institute', *A Witness and a Minister*, Memorial Number, 1933; cf. Brynmor Pierce Jones, *The King's Champions*, 214.
2. NLW, R. B. Jones Papers, Minor Collections, No. 41, testimony Gomer Jones.
3. Ibid., testimony William Jones.
4. Ibid., testimony Bronwen Hale.

5. 'The Bible Training School', *Yr Efengylydd*, November–December 1920.
6. Ibid.; 'The Story of what led to the School's Inception', *A Witness and a Minister*, 1925.
7. 'The Bible Training School', *Yr Efengylydd,* March–April, 1920.
8. NLW, R. B. Jones Papers, Minor Collections, No. 51.
9. Ibid.
10. Ibid.
11. 'The Bible Training School', *Yr Efengylydd*, November–December 1920.
12. 'Argraffiadau', *Yr Efengylydd*, March–April 1920.
13. NLW, R. B. Jones Papers, Minor Collections, No. 41, testimony of D. J. Williams.
14. Ibid., testimony of Menna Bowen, one of RB's daughters.
15. Ibid.
16. Ibid.
17. Ibid., testimony Bronwen Hale.
18. Ibid., testimony D. J. Williams.
19. Ibid., testimony Louisa Thornley.
20. Ibid., testimony T. J. Hughes.
21. Ibid., testimony Lumley Williams.
22. 'Nodion o'r Ysgol Feiblaidd', *Yr Efengylydd*, March 1922.
23. NLW, R. B. Jones Papers, Minor Collections, No. 41, testimony of Coplestone.
24. For Rees Howells: Norman Grubb, *Rees Howells, Intercessor* (1952, 1969).
25. 'Diwygiad Affricanaidd', *Yr Efengylydd*, February–March 1916; ibid., 'Diwygiad Rusitu', January 1917.
26. The author has made use of his chapter 'Pioneering at Porth' in *Taught to Serve* (Evangelical Press of Wales, 1986). The main source for that chapter was R. B. Jones Papers, Minor Collections, No. 18.
27. *Taught to Serve*, 24.
28. Introduction to a letter from R. B. Jones, 7 June 1923, that was included in *Yr Efengylydd*, giving an account of his journey in America, *Yr Efengylydd*, July 1923; ibid., 'Yr Ysgol Feiblaidd', August 1923.
29. R. B. Jones Papers, Minor Collections, No. 36.
30. *Taught to Serve*, 24.

31. *Taught to Serve*, 25-6.
32. Ibid., 26.
33. NLW, R. B. Jones Papers, Minor Collections, No. 18.
34. *Taught to Serve*, 28.
35. Ibid., 39 (56).
36. Ibid., 31.
37. Norman Grubb, *Rees Howells, Intercessor*, 198.
38. *Taught to Serve*, 31.
39. NLW, R. B. Jones Papers, Minor Collections, No. 31, July 1916.
40. Brynmor Pierce Jones, *The King's Champions*, 219.
41. 'Ysgol Feiblaidd y Porth', *Yr Efengylydd*, September 1925.
42. Ibid.
43. NLW, R. B. Jones Papers, Minor Collections, No. 18, letter 21 July 1926.
44. He was Courcy de Hamilton, who later supported the Barry Bible College: *Taught to Serve*, 73 (8).
45. Brynmor Pierce Jones, *The King's Champions*, 224.
46. Ibid., 226.
47. *A Witness and a Minister*, Memorial Number, 1933.
48. NLW, R. B. Jones Papers, Minor Collections, No. 41, testimony of Enid, one of RB's daughters.
49. 'Yr Athro Beiblaidd', *Yr Efengylydd,* 1933; 'The Bible Teacher', *A Witness and a Minister*, Memorial Number, 1933.
50. 'Annual Reports', *A Witness and a Minister*, September 1929.
51. NLW, R. B. Jones Papers, Minor Collections, No 41, testimony of Gordon Diamond.
52. 'Annual Reports', *A Witness and a Minister*, September 1929.
53. They produced a tract, introducing themselves as 'The Two Missionaries of the Faith Mission of Wales' and listing a number of points for prayer; personal copy.
54. Ibid.
55. Brynmor Pierce Jones, *The King's Champions*, 242.
56. Ibid.
57. NLW, R. B. Jones Papers, Minor Collections, No. 41, testimony of B. J. Allsop.
58. Ibid., testimony of Edward Hough.
59. Ibid., testimony of Jack Barkey.
60. Ibid., testimony of Bronwen Hale.
61. Later joined the staff at the Barry Bible College, and was on the

Council, *Taught to Serve*, 50, 51, 246.

62. T. M. Bassett, *The Baptists of Wales and the Baptist Missionary Society*, 56.
63. Brynmor Pierce Jones, *The King's Champions*, 290.
64. Noel Gibbard, *On the Wings of the Dove*, 66.
65. Ibid., 208.
66. 'The story of my life', *Yr Efengylydd*, April 1927.
67. Ibid.
68. 'Ysgol Feiblaidd y Porth', *Yr Efengylydd*, March 1927; *Church Manual and Record*, 1926. Some of the proceeds of the Weekly Bible Lecture were set aside for the support of students, and in 1927 an extra £27 was given to support a Russian student, ibid., 1927.
69. Michael Rowe, *Russian Resurrection* (1994), 79-80; Noel Gibbard, *On the Wings of the Dove*, 213.
70. *Yr Efengylydd*, March 1927.
71. Brynmor Pierce Jones, *The King's Champions*, 292.
72. D. M. Phillips, 'Y Parch R. B. Jones', *Y Goleuad*, 16 August 1933; NLW, R. B. Jones Papers, Minor Collections, No. 41, testimony Menna Bowen, one of RB's daughters.
73. NLW, R. B. Jones Papers, Minor Collections, No. 41, testimony Lumley Williams.
74. Ibid., testimony Charles Price.
75. Editorial, *Riches of Grace*, 1935.
76. 'Ymweliad y Dr Dick Wilson a'r Porth', *Yr Efengylydd*, August 1925.
77. Geoffrey Thomas, 'Gresham Machen in the United Kingdom', *Banner of Truth*, 1983.

Chapter 8

1. A later edition is used (*Overcomer*, n.d.); included with it: 'The Believer's Warfare' and 'The Believer's Service'.
2. *The Gospel for the Believer*, 1.
3. Ibid., 6-7.
4. Ibid., 11-12.
5. Ibid., 15-16.
6. Ibid., 13.
7. Ibid., 14.
8. Ibid., 15.

9. Ibid.
10. Ibid., 17.
11. Ibid., 20-1.
12. Ibid., 21.
13. Ibid., 22.
14. Ibid., 23.
15. Ibid., 23-4.
16. Ibid., 26.
17. *Christ Our Life*; the section 'The Life Root'.
18. Ibid., the section 'Life's Fetters Freed'.
19. Ibid., the section 'The Life Gift'.
20. Ibid., 'Life's Ideal', 39-40.
21. Ibid., section 'Nature of the Life'.
22. Ibid., section 'The Life Character'.
23. Ibid., 62.
24. Ibid., 'His saving life', 71.
25. Ibid., 66, 76.
26. Ibid., 80.
27. Ibid., sections: 'Life the goal' and 'Life the power'.
28. Ibid., 38-9.
29. Ibid., 15.
30. Ibid., 85-6.
31. *Arian ei Arglwydd*, 5, 7, 9.
32. Ibid., 8-10.
33. Ibid., 23-4.
34. Ibid., 33, 36.
35. Ibid., 33-8.
36. Ibid., 54-8.
37. Ibid., 58-60.
38. Ibid., 59.
39. Ibid., 70-80.
40. 'Ffordd y Pentecost', *Yr Efengylydd*, March 1925.
41. *Rent Heavens*, 13, 15.
42. Ibid., 15.
43. Ibid.
44. Ibid., 16.
45. Ibid., 23, 37, 43, 61, 63.
46. Ibid., 54.
47. Ibid., 43.

48. Geraint Jones, 'Dau Ddiwygiwr', *Seren Gomer*, Winter 1956; *Rent Heavens*, Ibid., 53.
49. NLW, Brynmor P. Jones, Research Papers, Minor Collections, No. 33.
50. *Rent Heavens*, 55.
51. Ibid., 31.
52. Ibid., 56-7.
53. Ibid., 81.
54. Ibid., chapter VI.
55. Ibid., 90-1.
56. 'Rhagarweiniad': XL-XLVI. For a very critical approach to the doctrine: R. S. Rogers, *Y Deyrnas a'r Ail Ddyfodiad* (Mountain Ash, 1914); more moderate approach: J. Puleston Jones, *Epistol Iago* (1898), *Until the Day Dawn* (1913).
57. 'Rhagarweiniad', XXXVII.
58. Ibid., LIII-LVIII.
59. *Yr Ail-Ddyfodiad yng Ngoleuni'r Epistolau at y Thesaloniaid:* Inter Linear, e.g. 10, 12, 23, and he could make use of the LXX as well, 71; Weymouth, 41, 85, Ellicott, 10, 26, 61, 77; Denney, 9, 13, 13, 23, 31, 34, 59, 75, 87; Findlay, 67, 73, 85; Revised Version, 22, 23, 41, 67, and on 22 and 41, refers to different MSS.
60. Ibid., 8.
61. RB would be aware of the teaching of Moody and Keswick, and had accepted premillennialism before Scofield's *Reference Bible* appeared in 1909, but Scofield presented the classical view of pre-millennialism.
62. Ibid., 17-20.
63. 'Y Deyrnas', *Yr Efengylydd*, June 1926.
64. Ibid., 'Dydd yr Arglwydd' (Day of the Lord), 40-1.
65. Ibid., 23-4.
66. Ibid., 26.

Chapter 9

1. *Dr T. R. Glover and the Presidency*, 3.
2. Ibid., 5.
3. Ibid., 6.
4. Ibid., 8, 10.
5. Ibid., 11.

6. Ibid., 14, 15.
7. Ibid., 12.
8. Ibid., 17, 18.
9. Ibid., 22.
10. Ibid., 20, 22.
11. NLW, R. B. Jones Papers, No. 41, testimony of Richard Russell; *Jubilee Souvenir*, 24.
12. *Jubilee Souvenir*, 24.
13. *Ibid.*, 25.
14. *Resolution Dr T. R. Glover and Presidency*, 3; resolution moved at Tabernacle, slightly different: *Jubilee Souvenir*, 24.
15. Ibid.
16. 'Undeb y Bedyddwyr Saesneg', *Seren Cymru*, 16 May 1924.
17. 'Llythyr agored at y Parch R. B. Jones', *Seren Cymru*, 30 May 1924.
18. Ibid., 'Undeb y Bedyddwyr Saesneg', 16 May 1924.
19. NLW, R. B. Jones Papers, Minor Collections, No. 4. Dr Mabie's works used by Jessie Penn-Lewis: *The Meaning and Message of the Cross, The Divine Reason of the Cross*, and *How does the death of Christ save us?*
20. Ibid.
21. Ibid.
22. *The Infallibility of the Man Jesus*, 3, 10.
23. *Bible Witness*, July 1924.
24. Ibid., 2-3.
25. *The Infallibility of the Man Jesus*, 7.
26. *The Infallibility of the Man Jesus*, 7-8.
27. Bible Union, 6.
28. *The Infallibility of the Man Jesus*, 15-16.
29. Ibid., 20.
30. Ibid., 24.
31. Ibid., 31.
32. Ibid., 32.
33. NLW, R. B. Jones Papers, No. 1, letter J. P. Wiles, 7 April 1925.
34. Ibid.
35. Ibid., 22.
36. RB's reply, 22 May 1925.
37. Ibid., letter 11:2:25.
38. Ibid., letter Feb. 3/25.
39. RB's reply, 22 May 1925.

40. 'Buchaniaeth', *Yr Efengylydd*, 1931.
41. *Spiritism in Bible Light*, 1.
42. Ibid., 3-5.
43. Ibid., 6-12, 17-23.
44. Ibid., 28-31.
45. Ibid., 31-2.
46. Ibid., 42, and the whole section, 39-43.
47. Ibid., 42-3.
48. Ibid., 85-96.
49. Ibid., 97-103.
50. Ibid., 183.
51. Ibid., 188.
52. Ibid., 189-190.
53. Ibid., 205.
54. Ibid.
55. Ibid., 206.
56. Ibid.

Chapter 10
1. 'The Revival at Ynyshir', *The Rhondda Leader,* 10 December 1904.
2. Examples in chapters 2 and 3.
3. Brynmor Pierce Jones, *The King's Champions*, 269.
4. NLW, copy included in R. B. Jones Papers, Minor Collections, No. 23; a notebook of Welsh Hymns composed or translated, ibid., No. 9. When W. S. Jones went to America in 1908, he took an enlarged edition with him.
5. Ibid., No. 41.
6. NLW, from R. B. Jones Papers, Minor Collections, No.9.
7. Appeared in *Yr Efengylydd*, April 1923; Brynmor Pierce Jones included it in *The King's Champions*, 279-80.

Chapter 11
1. Information from the late Geraint Jones, one of RB's sons.
2. 'Death of the Rev. R. B. Jones', *Porth Gazette*, 22 April 1933. NLW, R. B. Jones Papers, Minor Collections, No. 4, included: Gresham Machen, Eluned Morgan, Bishop Taylor Smith; Spanish

Gospel Mission, Sudan Interior Mission, Africa Inland Mission, Japan Rescue Mission.

3. Ibid., No. 36.
4. Examples of reports: 'Funeral of the Rev R. B. Jones', *Porth Gazette*; 'Angladd y Parch. R. B. Jones', *Seren Cymru*, 5 May 1933; 'Funeral of the Rev. R. B. Jones', *Free Press and Rhondda Leader*, 29 April 1933; T. Roberts, 'Miloedd yn talu gwrogaeth', *Yr Efengylydd*, 1933. English hymns at the funeral: 'There is a fountain filled with blood'; 'To Thee, and to Thy Christ, O God'; 'Just as I am, without one plea', and the Welsh hymns: 'Arnat Iesu boed fy meddwl', and 'Am Iesu Grist a'i farwol glwy': *Hymns to be sung at the funeral of Rev. R. B. Jones*, personal copy. A memorial service was held on the Wednesday afternoon of the 1933 Ammanford Convention, *Yr Efengylydd*, Memorial Number, 1933, 96.
5. Geraint Jones, 'R. B. Jones', *Seren Cymru*, 19 November 1943; ibid., 'R. B. Jones. A Son's Assessment', *Seren Cymru*, 10 October 1969.
6. *Witness and a Minister*, Memorial Number, 1933.
7. NLW, R. B. Jones Papers, Minor Collections, No. 35, testimony of Idris Davies.
8. Ibid., No. 41, testimony of Richard Russell.
9. Brynmor Pierce Jones, *The King's Champions*, 270; also 276.
10. Geraint Jones, 'R. B. Jones. A Son's Assessment', *Seren Cymru*, 10 October 1969.
11. Ibid., 17 October 1969.
12. Ibid., 10 October 1969. Herbert Morgan had told RB that 'to believe what my father believed would mean intellectual suicide', and RB responded by saying that 'to believe what Herbert Morgan believed would mean spiritual suicide', ibid. RB had refused to attend Herbert Morgan's ordination: D. Hugh Matthews, *Hanes Ty Cwrdd Castle Street* (Abertawe, 1989), 29, and quoted by Robert Pope, *Codi Muriau Dinas Duw* (2005), 127. But RB's financial support for Herbert Morgan and the Castle Street visit are further considerations to assess the relationship between RB and Herbert Morgan.
13. D. Ff. Dafis, 'Ysbrydoliaeth y Beibl', *Seren Cymru*, 27 April 1923; Edward Owen Jones, 'Y Beibl a Beirniadaeth', 3 August 1923.

14. Ibid.; NLW, R. B. Jones Papers, Minor Collections, No. 13.
15. Ibid.
16. *A Witness and a Minister*, Memorial Number, 1933.
17. Ibid.
18. NLW, R. B. Jones Papers, Minor Collections, No. 4.
19. Points mentioned by Geraint Jones in two articles, 'Dau Ddiwygiwr', *Seren Gomer*, Autumn, Winter, 1956.
20. NLW, R. B. Jones Papers, Minor Collections, 'Some Impressions', No. 35.
21. 'R. B. Jones, Porth', *Seren Gomer*, September 1939.
22. Ibid.
23. Quoted by O. M. Owen, 'Atgofion o'i Bererindod Ysbrydol', *Yr Efengylydd*, Memorial Number, 1933. And a testimony from the *Western Mail*: Brynmor P. Jones, Thesis, 354.
24. Geraint Jones, 'R. B. Jones. A Son's Assessment', *Seren Cymru*, 17 October 1969. And a testimony from the *Western Mail:* 'He gave us the essence of fundamentalism and an amazing exposition. What strikes you forcibly is the sheer sincerity, the colossal conviction, the vital earnestness to convince you and convert you into the beliefs which have absorbed his existence', quoted by Brynmor P. Jones, Thesis, 354.
25. NLW, R. B. Jones Papers, Minor Collections, No. 35.
26. O. M. Owen, 'Atgofion o'i Bererindod Ysbrydol', *Yr Efengylydd*, Memorial Number, 1933; Owen Thomas, a former student: 'We are reminded of his desire to have us preach at all times to men's consciences', *A Witness and a Minister*, Memorial Number; Geraint Jones, 'R. B. Jones', *Seren Cymru*, 29 October 1943.
27. 'Treasurer's Report', *Witness and a Minister*, October 1934.
28. Geraint Jones, 'A Son's Assessment', *Seren Cymru*, 17 October 1969.
29. April 1933; *Witness and a Minister*, Memorial Number, 1933.
30. *D. Martyn Lloyd-Jones, The First Forty Years 1899–1939* (The Banner of Truth Trust, 1982), 192-3.
31. Ibid.
32. Ibid., 193. There are only a few references to Charles Finney in *Yr Efengylydd* before 1919, but a number appeared during the 1920s and early 30s. The editors were hoping, perhaps, that Finney could help them to prepare for another revival. RB himself did not give any prominence to Finney.

33. NLW, R. B. Jones Papers, Minor Collections, No. 26.
34. Brynmor Pierce Jones, *The King's Champions*, 268-9.
35. NLW, R. B. Jones Papers, Minor Collections, No. 12. RB: 'I am completely indifferent to the results of Higher Criticism, the Book now lives and speaks to me and in the charm of its melodious sweetness and the wealth of its truths one forgets its garb, though perhaps in tatters from the thorns of criticism', ibid.
36. Geraint Jones to Gresham Machen, 5/10/33, copy received from Rev. Geoffrey Thomas, Aberystwyth.
37. *Witness and a Minister*, Memorial Number, 1933, 7.
38. Related by former student Owen Thomas to the Rev. Sulwyn Jones, Dowlais.

Index

Gray (Dr), 110, 120
Green, Samuel G., 120
Gregory, R. T., 129
Griffith, Gwilym O., 72
Griffith, J. T., 73
Griffiths, D. T., 133
Grubb, George, 84
Grubb, Norman, 126
Guest, Charlotte, 11, 14
Guest, John (Sir), 11, 14
Gwendraeth valley, 93, 106

H

Hale, Bronwen, 131-2
Hamilton, E. L., 80
Handbook of Christian Doctrine, 21, 25
Harlech, 60, 91
Harnack, Adolf, 79
Harris, Howell, 88, 185
Hart, T. W., 97
Hastings, 113
Havergal, Frances Ridley, 170
Hay, R. Wright, 107
Head, Albert, 28, 63, 64
Heavenly Sunlight, 169
Hebrew Christian Testimony, 132
Hebron, Dowlais, 11, 12, 13, 35, 38, 49, 85
Hidden Heroisms of Faith, 144
Hill, W. G., 90
Hinduism, 109
Hine, S. K., 133
His Lord's Money, *see Arian ei Arglwydd*
Holden, J. S., 30
Holiness, 183, 184, *see also* Sanctification
Hollins, Agnes, 89, 91
Hollywood, 111
Holyhead, 47, 51, 52, 85, 93
Holy Spirit, the, *see* Sanctification; Revival (in general)

Hopkin, David, 47
Hopkins, Evan, 29, 63, 67, 80
How to Study the Bible, 120
Howell (Dean), 28
Howells, George, 107, 108
Howells, Rees, 85, 89, 123-5, 126
Hughes, A. L., 132
Hughes, David, 88
Hughes, Griffith, 82, 91, 92, 93, 94, 106
Hughes, J. Cromwell, 74
Hughes, J. Williams, 117
Hyfforddwr Salem, 25
Hymns and hymn tunes, 169-75
Hymns of Consecration and Faith, 169, 171

I

India, 79, 107, 132
Infallibility of the Man Jesus Christ, The, 160-2
Inwood, Charles, 30, 63, 64, 66
Irenaeus, 164
Islam, 109

J

James, Joseph, 85
James, O. W., 15
James, W. R., 108
Japan Evangelistic Band, 106
Jeffreys, T. M., 126
Jenkins, Joseph, 54-5, 92
Jenkins, Sam, 72, 82, 90
Jenkyn, William, 120
Jerusalem, Ynys-hir, 62
Jesus of History, The, 157
John, May, 52
Johns, Thomas, 19
Jones, Arianwen, 114, 132, 133, 135
Jones, A. V. (Mrs), 129
Jones, Brynmor Pierce, 15, 16, 21, 26, 67, 75, 100

Jones, W. S. (Llwynypia), 19, 27,
28, 29, 32-3, 34, 45, 61-2, 67, 73,
77, 82, 84, 86, 87, 90, 97, 115,
119, 149, 181-2, 192
Jones, W. S. (Mrs), 119
Joshua, Seth, 72, 86, 90, 126
Joy of Bible Study, The, 120
Judson, Adoniram, 88

K

Kalvington (Mrs), 80, 81
Kehl, F. (India), 80, 81, 110
Keswick, 27, 28, 38, 63, 64, 66, 80,
83, 150
Keswick-in-Wales, 27, 28, 30, 83,
see also Llandrindod
King's Business, The, 102
Korea, 72

L

Latvia, 113-15, 132
Lecture, monthly, 103-5
Lecturers and helpers, *see under*
Bible Training School/Institute
Legge, Fred, 131
Leicester, 80
Lewis, Thomas, 79
Lewis, W. W., 54, 82, 84, 90, 92,
119, 120
Life of Faith, The, 67, 80
Litchfield, George, 80
Lithuania, 114
Liverpool, 58. 59, 191
Liverpool City Mission, 131
Llanarth, 92
Llanbadarn, 91
Llanberis, 56
Llanboidy, 69
Llandeilo, 91
Llandovery, 93
Llandrindod, 27-31, 35, 58, 62, 63,
64, 65, 67, 69, 81, 82, 85, 90, 91,
105, 123, 150, 181

Llandudno, 58, 61
Llanddeusant (Anglesey), 51
Llanelli, 18-19, 58, 59, 66, 82-3,
106, 113, 115, 133, 176
Llanfachreth, 51, 53
Llanfyllin, 91
Llangadog, 91
Llangefni, 51, 52, 54
Llangennech, 93
Llangollen, 58
Llangwyryfon, 92
Llanllyfni, 56
Llannerch-y-medd, 51, 52, 53
Llan-non, 54, 92
Llanrhystud, 92
Llantrisant, 130
Llawlyfr Moliant, 169, 173
Lloyd, David, 16, 47, 51, 52, 93
Lloyd George, 179
Lloyd-Jones, Martyn, 134-5, 176,
189
Llwynhendy, 77
Llwynypia, 32, 38, 65, 66, 67
Local church life, 36-7, 71-2
(Ainon, Ynys-hir); 98-103
(Tabernacle, Porth)
Lodge, Oliver, 166
London, 191
Long Island, 111
Los Angeles, 111
Loughor, 38, 40, 60
Luther, Martin, 164

M

Mabie (Dr), 160
Macdonald, J. I., 107
Machen, Gresham, 135, 136, 157
Mansfield (Miss), 68
McCaig (Dr), 114, 115, 186
McNeill, John, 135
Merthyr Tydfil, 38, 61
Metropolitan Tabernacle, London,
66, 113-14, 116, 186

Southern States of America, 111
Spanish Gospel Mission, 132
Spiritism in Bible Light, 104,
 164-8
Spurgeon, C. H., 32, 157, 186
Spurgeon's College, 132
St Paul, Minnesota, 116
Stephens, Thomas, 27
Studd, C. T., 115
Student evangelism, *see under*
 Bible Training School/Institute
Sunday, Billy, 116
Sunday School Hymns, 170
Sutherland, Sister, 97, 103, 110,
 124, 129
Swansea, 67, 81, 123, 124, 125,
 130, 176
Swansea Bible College, 112, 125-6

T

Tabernacle, Porth, 94, 95, 96-7, 98-
 103, 106, 109, 112-13, 116, 117,
 158, 176, 185, 190, *see also*
 Local church life
Tal-y-sarn, 56
Telyn Seion, 171
Telynor Seiriol, 52
Temple Chimes, 169
Thado-Kookie Mission, 110
Theological controversy, *see under*
 Jones, R. B.
Theology of the Old Testament, 43
Thomas, Ceinfryn, 16, 18, 25, 38
Thomas, Daniel (S. America), 89
Thomas, David, 96
Thomas, Esther, 130
Thomas, E. Ungoed, 107-8, 109
Thomas, Gwynhefin, 29, 115
Thomas, Huxley, 85
Thomas, John, 88, 107
Thomas, John (Liverpool), 125, 126
Thomas, John (Llandeilo), 130
Thomas, Owen, 193

Thomas, Owen (Liverpool), 187
Thomas, T. C., 72
Thomas, William James, 76
Thomas, W. H. Griffith, 120
Thornley, Louisa, 130
Toledo, 111
Tongwynlais, 106
Ton-mawr, 130
Tonypandy, 29
Tonyrefail, 61
Toronto, 116
Torrey, R. A., 39, 41-2, 110, 120,
 163
Trapp, John, 120
Trecynon, 38, 42, 49
Tredegar, 60
Trefforest, 61
Trehafod, 122, 130
Treharris, 17, 65, 120, 181
Treherbert, 56, 85
Trekking, *see under* Evangelism
Treorci, 34, 86
Trumbull, C. G., 111
Tynycymer Hall, Porth, 127, 136

U

United States, 72, *see also* America
Urban, George, 134

V

Vagar, Jacob, 134
Visiting speakers, *see under* Bible
 Training School/Institute

W

Watson, Sidney, 113, 129
Watts, Isaac, 170
Weaver, Frank, 45
Wesley, Charles, 170
Wesley, John, 186
Weymouth, R .F., 153
What is Christianity? 136
What the Bible Teaches, 163